# Unlocking Wiccan Mysteries and Spirituality

## Sacred Whispers: Embracing the Mysticism and Spiritual Practices of Wicca

**Isabella Knight**

# Table of Contents

# INTRODUCTION

Discover the unique journey of "Unlocking Wiccan Mysteries and Spirituality: Sacred Whispers: Embracing the Mysticism and Spiritual Practices of Wicca." This isn't just another guide-it's a transformative experience. With its blend of ancient wisdom and contemporary relevance, Wicca is a nature-based spiritual practice that invites you on a life-changing adventure guided by the heart of this book. No matter your experience level, this guide is designed to deepen your understanding of Wiccan beliefs, ceremonies, and the profound connection between spirituality and the natural world.

Wicca, which is frequently misinterpreted and misunderstood, has its roots in respect for the Earth, the seasonal cycles, and the equilibrium of energies. By delving into its foundational principles, holy writings, and an array of gods, you will uncover the enchanted fabric of Wicca. With the knowledge in this book, you can create your own Book of Shadows and significant rituals based on the Wheel of the Year, Esbats, Spellcraft, and the use of magical equipment.

More than just a manual, "Unlocking Wiccan Mysteries and Spirituality" extends an invitation to adopt a lifestyle focused on spiritual development, mindfulness, and reverence for the natural world. Allow Wicca's holy humor to beckon you to delve deeper into its mysteries and incorporate its practices into your everyday existence, cultivating a more profound relationship with both the cosmos and you.

# CHAPTER I

# Origins and Evolution

## Ancient roots and influences

As a modern spiritual movement, Wicca has ancient roots and influences that cut across centuries and cultural boundaries. Gaining an appreciation of the richness and variety of Wiccan practices and beliefs requires an understanding of their historical underpinnings. Wicca's rich and complex character is woven from the threads of primordial paganism, classical antiquity, medieval witchcraft traditions, and contemporary esoteric philosophy.

The origins of Wicca can be found in prehistoric paganism, a religion in which a significant component of human spirituality was nature worship. The Venus figurines and other fertility symbols, among other archeological discoveries, indicate that early human communities worshipped and deified natural cycles. Seasonal rituals and animistic beliefs were among the ancient traditions that established the foundation for many of the themes seen in contemporary Wicca. Wicca today is deeply resonant with the ideals of reverence for the Earth and the cyclical nature of life, death, and rebirth.

The elements that would subsequently impact Wicca are further developed in classical antiquity. Pantheons of gods and goddesses representing different facets of nature and the human experience existed in the pantheons of ancient civilizations like the Greeks and Romans. Wicca's initiatory traditions emphasize personal spiritual experiences and initiations in these mystery religions, especially those of Eleusis and Dionysus. The Hermetic books, which began in Hellenistic Egypt, also brought concepts of alchemy, magic, and the relationship between the macrocosm and microcosm. Wicca is one of the Western esoteric systems that these Hermetic ideas have dramatically impacted.

Wiccan ideas were further developed during the medieval era due to European folklore and witchcraft customs. Even though Christianity was becoming the most popular religion then, rural villages frequently held onto remnants of their previous pagan customs. Herbal medicine, folk magic, and the adoration of regional deities or spirits endured differently. From these beliefs arose the figure of the "witch," frequently a wise lady or healer. The history surrounding witches has been incorporated into Wiccan identity, recovering and reinterpreting the witch archetype as a strong and kind figure, even if the persecution of witches during the witch hunts was motivated more by fear and superstition than by actual actions.

Ancient knowledge and esoteric traditions enjoyed a resurgence of interest throughout the Renaissance and the Enlightenment. Hermeticism, Neoplatonism, and other occult systems were studied and revitalized by academics and mystics like John Dee and Marsilio Ficino. Grimoires, or books of magic and ritual, were also published. The combination of various occult traditions created the theoretical framework for the magical rituals that became part of Wicca.

The 19th and early 20th centuries saw the rise of numerous significant movements and individuals, making this a pivotal time in the development of contemporary Wicca. New spiritual traditions flourished because the Romantic movement concerned nature, the paranormal, and the resurgence of interest in folklore and ancient faiths. The writings of folklorists such as Sir James Frazer, the author of "The Golden Bough," brought attention to the similarities between traditional fertility rites and modern activities, implying that paganism has not changed.

Gerald Gardner is the most critical person in developing Wicca as a logical spiritual path. Gardner combined many aspects of folklore, occultism, and ceremonial magic in the middle of the 20th century to create what is now known as Wicca. Although there is disagreement over the historical veracity of Gardner's claim to have been initiated into a coven of surviving witches, his writings and practices have significantly influenced the development of modern Wicca. Aleister Crowley's writings, which focused on ceremonial aspects of the occult and ritual magic, significantly influenced Gardner's Wicca. Many of the central Wicca rituals, beliefs, and structures were founded by the Gardnerian tradition, as it came to be known.

Other influential people and traditions also influenced the evolution of Wicca. Known as the "Mother of Modern Witchcraft," Doreen Valiente significantly influenced the development of Wiccan rituals and liturgy, placing particular emphasis on the Goddess and poetry. The diversity within Wicca today results from Raymond Buckland and Alex Sanders' dissemination of Wiccan concepts, who each added their interpretations and practices.

In summary, Wicca's ancient roots and influences are a patchwork of ancient paganism, classical esotericism, medieval folklore, Renaissance esotericism, and contemporary occultism. The rich legacy of Wicca provides Wiccan spirituality with a deep connection to the past and a dynamic, ever-evolving path for modern practitioners; an appreciation of these influences enables us to recognize the richness of Wiccan practice and its place in the larger context of spiritual history.

## Key historical figures

Wicca is a contemporary spiritual path influenced and enhanced by several significant historical people whose contributions have been essential to its growth and acceptance. These people have contributed to defining the characteristics of modern Wicca by fusing antiquated customs with current sensibilities through their publications, rituals, and engaging personalities. Gerald Gardner, Doreen Valiente, Aleister Crowley, Raymond Buckland, and Alex Sanders are a few of the most critical individuals. Each of these people has made a lasting contribution to Wicca's rituals, philosophies, and organizational frameworks.

Many people consider Gerald Gardner to be the founder of contemporary Wicca. Born in 1884, Gardner has a lifelong fascination with occultism, magic, and folklore. After retiring from the British colonial service, he dedicated his time to researching and bringing back historical pagan customs. Gardner made the controversial but unquestionably significant allegation that he was initiated into a coven of witches in the New Forest in 1939. His publications, such as "Witchcraft Today" (1954) and "The Meaning of Witchcraft" (1959), helped establish the groundwork for contemporary Wiccan rituals. Ritual magic, deity worship, and a code of ethics called the Wiccan Rede were all central to Gardner's Wicca. The expansion and acceptance of Wicca in the middle of the 20th century was greatly aided by his attempts to make it known and legitimate it as a profound spiritual path.

Known as the "Mother of Modern Witchcraft," Doreen Valiente significantly influenced the rituals and practices of the Wiccan faith. Gardner first encountered poet and occultist Valiente, born in 1922, in the early 1950s. She rose swiftly through the ranks of Gardner's coven to the position of high priestess, working alongside him to create many of the writings and rituals now essential to Wiccan life. The poetic and evocative language of Wiccan ceremonies was crafted by Valiente, whose ability for poetry made them more meaningful and approachable. Among her contributions is the seminal work "Charge of the Goddess," which briefly summarizes the Wicca spiritual cosmology. Wicca, as envisioned by Valiente, was a practical and mystical art that strongly emphasized nature's holiness and individual empowerment.

Despite not being a Wiccan, Aleister Crowley's contributions to occult thought and practice significantly influenced the growth of modern Wicca. Crowley, born in 1875, was a prolific writer, magician, and the creator of the Thelema religious ideology. Many occultists of his age were affected by his emphasis on ceremonial magic, individual willpower, and the investigation of mystical experiences, among them Gerald Gardner. Gardnerian Wicca resembles Crowley's rituals and magical practices, especially regarding the design and symbolism of Wiccan ceremonies. The foundation Crowley's writings offered for comprehending and using magic has been modified and included in Wiccan customs.

Another influential person in the Wicca movement, especially in the US, is Raymond Buckland. Gardner's writing greatly impacted Buckland; an American of British descent born in 1934. Following his studies with Gardner in the 1960s, Buckland founded the first Gardnerian coven in America, bringing Gardnerian Wicca to the United States. Several works on Wicca and witchcraft have been written by him, notably the immensely popular "Buckland's Complete Book of Witchcraft" (1986). Through his works, Buckland made Wicca accessible to a broader audience by thoroughly explaining the practice. In addition, he stressed the need for eclecticism and individual adaptation in Wicca, encouraging practitioners to discover their route within the larger tradition.

Known as the "King of the Witches," Alex Sanders was another well-known member of the Wiccan community. Born in 1926, Sanders created the Alexandrian Wicca lineage in the 1960s, fusing his innovations and personal rituals with aspects of Gardnerian Wicca. Wicca gained popularity partly thanks to Sanders's theatrical public rites and captivating personality. He took a more ceremonial and structured approach to Wicca, emphasizing formal training and ritual magic. Although the Alexandrian tradition shared many similarities with Gardnerian Wicca, it also included new components and variations that expanded the scope of Wiccan practice.

In conclusion, critical historical individuals, including Gerald Gardner, Doreen Valiente, Aleister Crowley, Raymond Buckland, and Alex Sanders, have substantially influenced Wicca's growth and popularization. Each of these people contributed distinctive ideas and viewpoints to Wicca, assisting in developing a dynamic and changing spiritual path that embraces contemporary understanding while paying homage to long-standing customs. Their legacy has influenced and continues to impact Wiccans worldwide, creating a vibrant and diverse community committed to delving into the secrets of the natural and supernatural worlds.

## The modern revival of Wicca

The intriguing story of Wicca's modern resurgence describes how a naturalistic, age-old spiritual tradition has evolved into a vibrant, modern movement via rediscovery, adaptation, and evolution. In the middle of the 20th century, this resurgence resulted from a confluence of historical curiosity, academic research, individual inquiry, and the prevailing cultural currents. The resurgence of Wicca as a prominent spiritual path has been primarily made possible by essential individuals, social movements, and knowledge sharing through books and media.

Gerald Gardner's significant role in the present rebirth of Wicca cannot be fully acknowledged in the text. Gardner was an amateur folklorist and retired British civil servant who claimed to have been admitted into a covert coven of witches in the New Forest in the 1940s and 1950s. Whether or whether Gardner's assertions are factual to history, his later deeds played a significant role in popularizing Wicca. He introduced Wicca as a respectable, old-fashioned religion with origins in pre-Christian Europe in his ground-breaking works "Witchcraft Today" (1954) and "The Meaning of Witchcraft" (1959). Gardner created a coherent framework for Wicca by combining ceremonial magic, modern pagan traditions, and folklore. This framework emphasized the worship of God and Goddess, seasonal festival celebrations, and ritual magic practice.

Another important person who worked closely with Gardner was Doreen Valiente, who enormously impacted Wiccan practice's poetry and liturgical aspects. The creation of the "Charge of the Goddess," still a key document in Wiccan rites, was one of Valiente's accomplishments. Her labor guaranteed that Wicca's rituals were meaningful, approachable, and evocative, contributing to a stronger sense of spiritual and mystical ties within the community. Wicca became an even more credible and alluring spiritual path because of Valiente's writings and campaigning, especially for people seeking alternatives to traditional religious activities.

An important factor in the resurgence of Wicca was undoubtedly the cultural and social movements of the 1960s and 1970s. Growing interest in alternative lifestyles, spiritual research, and countercultural values throughout this period made Wicca a flourishing practice. Wicca's emphasis on women's liberation and the divine feminine resonated particularly with the feminist movement. Wicca's spiritual framework, which revered female divinity and gave opportunities for leadership and personal development through its rituals and practices, drew many women to it.

The environmental movement also aided Wicca's popularity. Wicca's reverence for the Earth and its cycles offered a spiritual response that matched environmentalist beliefs as concerns about ecological degradation and the desire for a more harmonious interaction with nature grew. The Sabbats, which indicate the epochs of the solar year, and the Esbats, which commemorate the moon phases, are significant occasions for Wiccans to celebrate and establish connections with nature.

Book and media transmission of knowledge hastened the resurgence of Wicca even more. Wiccan traditions became more widely known thanks to the writings of authors like Silver Raven Wolf, Scott Cunningham, and Raymond Buckland. Cunningham's "Wicca: A Guide for the Solitary Practitioner" (1988) and Buckland's "Complete Book of Witchcraft" (1986) were especially significant since they offered helpful advice and encouraged people to investigate Wicca according to their terms. These books, with periodicals, TV shows, and later the internet, were essential in disseminating Wiccan beliefs and practices, facilitating the development of a varied and dispersed Wiccan community.

Another factor in the resurgence and expansion of Wicca was the creation of official Wiccan networks and organizations. Covens frequently provided controlled venues for practice and learning in the Gardnerian or Alexandrian traditions. Through initiation, instruction, and community, these groups contributed to transmitting and preserving Wiccan beliefs. In the meantime, isolated practitioners, encouraged by the availability of knowledge, developed their distinct rituals and interpretations, adding to the diversity of Wicca.

The internet transformed how Wiccan knowledge was shared and communities formed in the late 20th and early 21st centuries. Wiccans worldwide could communicate, exchange resources, and support one another through social media platforms, websites, and online forums. The advent of digital connectedness has facilitated the growth of Wicca as an international spiritual movement that cuts over national and cultural barriers.

Wicca's modern resurgence is evidence of the adaptability and tenacity of spiritual traditions. It expresses a deep desire to be in touch with the divine, the natural world, and oneself. Wicca has developed into a dynamic, living tradition that uplifts and empowers people worldwide by fusing antiquated customs with modern principles and ideas. With a foundation in the age-old respect for the sanctity of life and the natural world, Wicca continues to be a vibrant and welcoming path open to innovation.

# CHAPTER II

# Core Beliefs and Ethics

## The Wiccan Rede

A critical ethical declaration and tenet of Wicca, the Wiccan Rede is frequently summed up as "An it harm none, do what ye will." This brief but insightful aphorism captures the essence of Wiccan ethics and offers a guide for moral decision-making within the faith. Originating from the Middle English word for "advice" or "counsel," the Rede strongly emphasizes individual accountability, liberty, and the interdependence of all living things. Studying the Wiccan Rede's history, interpretations, and practical applications is necessary to comprehend it fully.

Although the Wiccan Rede's exact beginnings are unknown, Doreen Valiente, a pivotal figure in the evolution of contemporary Wicca, is frequently credited with formulating it. In the 1950s, Valiente, a well-known poet and high priestess, collaborated closely with Gerald Gardner. She made a substantial contribution to Wiccan philosophy and liturgy, and it is said that she assisted in crafting the Rede, which serves as a summary of Wiccan ethics. The maxim "An it harm none, do what ye will" is reminiscent of earlier moral precepts found in Western esoteric traditions, such as Aleister Crowley's well-known proclamation that "Do what thou wilt shall be the whole of the Law," with the qualification that "Love is the law, love under will." The Wiccan Rede clearly emphasizes the principle of non-harm, which is more in line with a broader ethical concern for the well-being of people and the natural world than Crowley's dictum, which emphasizes individual will and love.

To understand the Wiccan Rede, one must examine its two main parts: the command to "harm none" and the lenient sentence to "do what ye will." The command to "harm none" is a request to think about how one's activities affect others, the environment, and oneself. It calls on Wiccans to behave with mindfulness, compassion, and reverence for the interwoven web of life. This part of the Rede is consistent with Wicca's view of the sanctity of all life and the Earth's natural cycles. It serves as a reminder that everything you do has an impact and that leading an ethical life means being conscious of those effects.

The second half of the Rede, "Do what ye will," emphasizes the importance of individual autonomy and self-expression within the parameters established by the first phrase. This Rede component is consistent with Wicca's emphasis on personal spiritual development and independence. As long as they do it without causing harm, Wiccans are encouraged to follow their inner direction, forge their pathways, and pursue their goals. The equilibrium between liberty and accountability characterizes Wiccan ethics, cultivating a setting where moral behavior and individual empowerment coexist.

The Wiccan Rede is not just a philosophical concept, but a practical guide that significantly influences the daily lives and spiritual practices of Wiccans. It serves as a moral compass, guiding decisions about actions, relationships, and customs. For example, when practicing spell craft and magic, Wiccans ensure that their intentions and actions do not harm others, keeping the Rede in mind. This ethical consideration extends to all aspects of life, including interactions with communities and the treatment of the environment.

The Rede also greatly influences the manner in which Wiccans handle disputes and difficulties. The Rede's emphasis on non-harm urges Wiccans to look for amicable and constructive solutions and to settle disagreements by communication and understanding rather than by force or retaliation. This idea encourages empathy and compassion, strengthening people's bonds and building a cohesive community.

The Wiccan Rede's influence extends beyond personal ethics to environmental ethics, reflecting Wicca's strong connection to the natural world. The command to 'harm none' encompasses not only humans but also plants, animals, and the planet itself. Wiccans often engage in rituals that promote conservation, environmental sustainability, and reverence for nature. The Rede's ethical framework is directly mirrored in this ecological awareness, which underscores the importance of living in harmony with the environment.

The Wiccan Rede is a guiding concept that calls for careful interpretation and application rather than a set of inflexible rules. To resolve ethical problems, Wiccans are urged to rely on their judgment and intuition, understanding that difficult situations frequently call for situation-specific and nuanced solutions. Because of its adaptability and relevance in various settings, the Rede helps Wiccans make moral choices consistent with their beliefs and situation.

To sum up, the Wiccan Rede is a fundamental component of Wiccan ethics, encompassing the ideas of personal autonomy and non-harm within a framework of accountability and awareness. Its relevance as a guiding ethical statement is highlighted by its roots in the cooperative activity of early Wiccan individuals and its resonances with other esoteric traditions. Wiccans worldwide are influenced by the Rede's emphasis on compassion, autonomy, and ecological consciousness, which are fundamental Wiccan ideals. The Wiccan Rede is a living, breathing principle that inspires and challenges practitioners to live morally and authentically while respecting the interconnection of all life.

## The Threefold Law

A critical ethical tenet of Wicca is the Threefold Law, sometimes called the Law of Return. It states that any energy an individual expends on the world—positive or negative—will be tripled back to them. This idea is fundamental to Wiccan philosophy and acts as a robust moral code that encourages practitioners to act honorably, compassionately, and mindful of the effects of their choices. Though exclusive to Wicca, the Threefold Law is comparable to other spiritual traditions emphasizing the karmic consequences of deeds, emphasizing the common human comprehension of moral reciprocity.

Although the Threefold Law's exact beginnings are unknown, it is generally accepted that Gerald Gardner, the creator of contemporary Wicca, popularized it in the middle of the 20th century. The Threefold Law became one of the central tenets of Wicca after Gardner's writings and teachings helped to formalize many aspects of the religion. The Western occult tradition and earlier esoteric and mystical traditions, such as Hermeticism, which frequently discuss the connection between deeds and their consequences, are potential sources of inspiration for the principle. According to Gardner's theory, the Threefold Law served as a tool to uphold moral conduct and highlight the significance of good intentions and deeds.

It is necessary to interpret the Threefold Law's two facets —the qualitative and quantitative return on energy. The qualitative element postulates that the nature of the repercussions that follow will depend on the character of one's acts, whether good or bad. For example, deeds of compassion and kindness will evoke good memories, but deeds of malice or injury will have the opposite effect. This promotes an ethical and caring culture by encouraging Wiccans to know the caliber of their words, deeds, and thoughts.

There are several ways to understand the quantitative part of the Threefold Law, which states that there will be a threefold return on energy. Some Wiccans interpret this literally, thinking that one's deeds will have a threefold multiplicity of effects. Some interpret the "threefold" idea more figuratively, believing it to indicate that an individual's activities have a compounding effect that affects their bodily, emotional, and spiritual wellbeing. This amplification is a powerful reminder of the far-reaching consequences of our choices and the significance of leading morally upright lives.

The Threefold Law significantly impacts Wicca's use of magic and spellcraft. It is advised that practitioners carefully weigh the possible results of their magical operations to ensure that their activities are not harmful and have good intentions. This moral code encourages accountability in Wiccans and works to stop magic from being abused. Wiccans frequently incorporate statements or rituals in their spells that expressly declare their intention to do no harm and to behave in the highest good. The Wiccan ethic of respect for all living things and the interconnection of all things is in line with this attention in magical practice.

The Triple Law affects daily conduct and judgment even outside the magic domain. Wiccans are urged to lead moral lives, show compassion and respect to others, and think about how their actions affect the larger picture of the world. As practitioners understand that their actions contribute to the overall wellbeing of their families, communities, and the natural world, this principle develops a sense of community and connectivity. Individuals and society may experience greater harmony and fulfillment when prioritizing positive energy and moral behavior.

The spiritual aspect of the Threefold Law is also essential, as it shapes the way Wiccans perceive the universe and their connection to the divine. It emphasizes that there is a vast, linked web of life and that everything we do impacts the universe. This viewpoint fosters a sense of personal accountability for one's spiritual development, humility, and respect for the natural world. Wiccans seek to connect more deeply with their spiritual journey by equating themselves with the divine powers of harmony and balance through observance of the Threefold Law.

Crucially, the Threefold Law emphasizes purposeful life and the natural repercussions of one's actions rather than fostering a dread of retaliation. Wiccans are empowered to make deliberate decisions because they are aware of their choices' profound and wide-ranging consequences. This idea is also consistent with the immense Wiccan belief in the sanctity of life and the necessity of living in harmony with the cycles and rhythms of the natural world.

To sum up, the Threefold Law is a fundamental component of Wiccan ethics, highlighting the mutual nature of deeds and their results. It is a potent behavioral manual that inspires Wiccans to behave honorably, morally, and mindfully. Encouraging moral behavior and conscientious magic, the Threefold Law cultivates an environment of deference, empathy, and unity. It emphasizes the significance of living in harmony with the natural world and the divine, having an impact that goes beyond individual acts to a broader spiritual perspective. The Threefold Law serves as a compass that encourages and challenges Wiccans to live conscious, purposeful lives that enhance the wellbeing of all.

## Concepts of karma and balance

Like many other spiritual traditions, Wicca bases her knowledge of the universe's nature and moral behavior on karma and balance. Despite having their origins in Eastern philosophy, these ideas have been adopted and modified by Wicca to represent the particular ideals and worldviews of the religion. According to karma, the law of cause and effect, the energy a person expends on the world will eventually return to them, shaping their experiences and circumstances in the future. This idea emphasizes how all creatures are related to one another and how each person is accountable for their acts. Karma is frequently understood in Wicca as a type of moral responsibility, inspiring practitioners to conduct morally upright, considerate, and kind lives in all spheres.

In Wiccan philosophy, balance is strongly associated with karma, reflecting the value placed on harmony and balance in the natural world. Wiccans see the cosmos as a dynamic, ever-evolving interaction of opposing energies, such as light and dark, masculine and feminine, and development and decay. Balance is crucial to keep the universe stable and orderly and prevent any force from dominating others. This idea is mirrored in the Wiccan conception of the God and Goddess, who jointly represent the active and passive, the creative and destructive, and who cooperate to keep the world going.

Karma and balance are two ideas used in Wiccan practice in various ways to direct moral behavior and spiritual development. By acting according to the Wiccan Rede, "An it harm none, do what ye will," which emphasizes non-harm and personal responsibility, practitioners are encouraged to develop positive karma. Wiccans believe that by being kind, respectful, and compassionate to others, they can generate good energy that will be given back to them in kind, improving both their well-being and the community's general well-being.

Furthermore, Wiccans work to keep their spiritual practices and lives balanced since they understand that an unbalanced state can result in stagnation and discord. This entails seeking harmony within oneself and with the environment, respecting the cycles of nature, and realizing the interconnection of all things. Symbols and actions that encourage equilibrium are frequently included in rituals and ceremonies. Examples include the casting of circles, the calling forth of elemental energies, and the celebration of seasonal festivals. Through these rituals, Wiccans aim to harmonize their energies with the higher powers of creation and metamorphosis and tune into the cycles of the natural world.

Karma and balance are also very important in Wiccan magic and spellcraft. Practitioners are aware that the energy they summon and channel through magical processes can profoundly affect other people and themselves. Therefore, Wiccans are urged to think carefully about the moral implications of their spells and ensure that their goals are consistent with good growth and non-harm values. Wiccans aim to realize their aspirations while respecting the interdependence of all life by cooperating with the natural cycles and the universal rules of karma and balance.

Beyond specific deeds and magical processes, Wiccans' larger view of the cosmos and their role in it is shaped by the ideas of karma and balance. Wiccans understand that they are a part of a vast and complex web of existence in which every action, word, and thought has cosmic repercussions. Wiccans aim to develop a sense of connectivity, consciousness, and responsibility that transcends the self by living according to balance and karma. By doing this, they hope to further society's welfare and establish a planet in balance with nature's cycles and rhythms.

Karma and balance are essential to Wiccan theory and practice since they direct moral conduct, spiritual development, and magical processes. Adhering to these tenets, Wiccans aim to foster positive energy, preserve internal and external balance, and advance the welfare of all living things. Wiccans work to live in accordance with the universe's fundamental laws and create a harmonious, balanced, and full of good energy via awareness, compassion, and a profound reverence for the interconnectedness of all life.

# CHAPTER III

# Deities and Pantheons

## The God and Goddess

Since the beginning of time, the idea of gods and goddesses has been essential to human culture and civilization. These supernatural beings, who represent diverse facets of the natural world, the human condition, and the universe, have significantly impacted the development of cultural standards, religious beliefs, and social behaviors in various countries. The pantheon of divine beings is as varied as it is fascinating, ranging from the towering gods of ancient Greece and Rome to the revered gods and goddesses of Hinduism and the symbolic characters in numerous indigenous cultures.

Greek mythology depicted gods and goddesses as vital, frequently irrational entities that oversaw various spheres of existence. Zeus, the monarch of the gods, commanded thunder and the sky, signifying strength and authority. His spouse, Hera, was the goddess of family and marriage, representing the sacredness of these establishments. Other notable gods were Athena, the goddess of war and wisdom, who stood for bravery and strategic thinking, and Poseidon, the god of the sea, whose moods could produce calm or stormy waves. Greek mythology was relevant and complete with moral teachings because the gods were seen as having human-like features but superhuman powers and immortality. They were also given human emotions and defects.

Parallel to this, Greek traditions greatly influenced Roman mythology, which included a pantheon of gods and goddesses with similar traits but distinct names and slightly different attributes. Jupiter was the Roman equivalent of Zeus, while his consort, Juno, reflected Hera. Mars, the god of battle, had a special place in Roman culture because of the military nature of the empire. Venus, the goddess of beauty and love, was a significant figure in many tales, representing the force of attraction and desire. To further emphasize their value on family and domestic life, the Romans also worshiped Vesta, the goddess of the hearth and home.

Hinduism has a comprehensive and intricate conception of gods and goddesses, consisting of a large pantheon of gods representing many facets of the cosmos and the human condition. The central tenet of Hinduism is the existence of Brahman, the ultimate reality that takes on various forms. The three main gods, or Trimurti, are Shiva, the destroyer; Vishnu, the preserver; and Brahma, the creator. There are many avatars and consorts of these gods, all of whom are essential deities in their own right— for instance, hnu's incarnations, such as Rama and Krishna. H are crucial characters in Hindu epics. Devotioninduism also places a strong emphasis on goddess worship, with figures such as Durga, the warrior goddess who battles destructive forces, Saraswati, the goddess of education and the arts, and Lakshmi, the goddess of wealth and prosperity, all having enormous significance in religious rituals and mythology.

Rich traditions of gods and goddesses, each specifically reflecting their surroundings, beliefs, and values, are also found in indigenous communities worldwide. Native American theology strongly emphasizes a close relationship with nature by having deities personify animals and natural elements. For example, the Changing Woman is a crucial character in Navajo tradition, signifying fertility, development, and life. Maasaw, the protector of the Earth and the underworld, is revered by the Hopi people. The deities, as mentioned above, are intricately woven into the customs and ceremonies of their tribes, providing direction for their perception of the universe and their place in it.

Gods and goddesses are also important in traditional African faiths, frequently associated with natural events and ancestral spirits. For instance, the Yoruba religion has a pantheon known as the Orishas, each responsible for overseeing a specific facet of nature and life. Oshun, the goddess of rivers and love, represents fertility and sensuality, while Shango, the god of thunder and lightning, represents strength and justice. The intricate rites, dances, and ceremonies used to honor these deities reflect African spirituality's communal and participatory aspect.

In all these varied traditions, gods and goddesses represent the ideals, anxieties, hopes, and dreams of the communities who worship them. They provide moral frameworks and guiding principles and a way to explain the mysteries of life and the cosmos. These celestial beings transmit ageless lessons and cultural knowledge via myths and tales, guaranteeing their lasting imprint in the fabric of human history. Whether considered as actual entities, symbolic depictions, or psychological archetypes, the gods and goddesses continue to play a crucial role in the human search for purpose and connection in a constantly shifting universe.

## Common deities in Wiccan practice

Wicca is a contemporary paganism that emphasizes nature worship, moon cycles, and the adoration of a divine duality represented by the God and Goddess. This spirituality involves the devotion of a wide range of deities from diverse pantheons and is based on parts of ancient pagan traditions. Nonetheless, a few common deities that represent this nature-based religion's basic ideas and ideals are essential to Wiccan practice. These gods are frequently viewed as archetypes, standing in for more general ideas rather than specific historical individuals.

The dual nature of the God and the Goddess, viewed as complementary powers representing various facets of essence and existence, lies at the core of Wiccanism. The Triple Goddess, also known as the Maiden, the Mother, and the Crone, are the three phases of the moon and the phases of a woman's life that she holds. The Maiden symbolizes youth, fresh starts, and the waxing moon. She is frequently connected to inspiration, fertility, and springtime. The Mother reflects elements of maternity, creativity, and the harvest; she is a sign of maturity, nurturing, and the full moon. The Crone, associated with the waning moon, stands for understanding, metamorphosis, and the conclusion of cycles; it embodies the lessons gained from past experiences and the groundwork for fresh starts.

In Wiccan tradition, the Horned God is a typical representation of God, signifying vigor, the wilderness, and the life-death-rebirth cycle. He represents nature's wild, unadulterated parts and is connected to the sun, trees, and animals. Usually shown with antlers or horns, the Horned God emphasizes his affinity for animals and the natural environment. As the Goddess' opposite regarding nurturing and life-giving attributes, he symbolizes the seasons, especially the cycle of development and decay. He also plays a role in death and regeneration.

Wiccans may venerate deities from several mythologies in addition to the primary God and Goddess, including these characters in their rituals and spiritual practices. For example, many Wiccans honor Celtic mythological figures like Brigid and Cernunnos. The ancient Irish goddess Brigid is connected to smithcraft, fire, poetry, and healing. She is frequently called upon at Imbolc, a springtime celebration representing rebirth and creativity. The Celtic

God with horns, Cernunnos, is associated with the forest, animals, and fertility. He symbolizes plenty frequently associated with the Wiccan Horned God, representing the life energy and connection to the natural world.

Wiccan rituals sometimes integrate Greek and Roman deities. For instance, the moon, feral animals, and the hunt are all connected to the goddess Artemis, also known as Diana in Roman mythology. She is appropriate for Wiccan ceremonies that revolve around the moon and nature since she represents power, independence, and the natural world. Similarly, the god Apollo is sometimes revered for his association with light, wisdom, and healing. Apollo is connected to the sun, music, and prophesy.

Another important figure in Wicca is the Greek goddess Hecate, who stands for witchcraft, magic, and forks in the path. In Wiccan rituals, Hecate is frequently called upon for protection, divination, and wisdom when negotiating the mysteries of the unknown. She closely links herself with the Wiccan emphasis on the cyclical aspect of life and the investigation of the spiritual realm, given her associations with the moon and the underworld.

Egyptian mythology is another source of inspiration for Wiccans, who emphasize gods like Osiris and Isis. The goddess of magic, childbirth, and fertility, Isis, is revered for her nurturing and protective attributes. She is frequently called upon in ceremonies that ask for power, healing, and direction. Her consort, Osiris, embodies ideas of death and rebirth that are profoundly ingrained in Wiccan beliefs. He is linked to the afterlife, resurrection, and natural cycles.

Wicca's inclusive and eclectic aspect is reflected in the range of deities practiced within the faith. Wiccans accept a flexible and individualized approach to spirituality, allowing practitioners to connect with the deities that most strongly resonate with their own experiences and ideals rather than adhering to rigid dogmas. One of the things that makes Wicca unique is its ability to change and yet be relevant in the contemporary world.

To summarize, common deities in Wiccan practice comprise various figures drawn from many mythologies, each representing a unique part of the natural world, life, and the universe. The God and Goddess, whose duality stands for the harmony and interdependence of all things, are the central figures in this pantheon. Wiccans worship these deities to honor life cycles, become more in sync with nature, and access the ancient wisdom these holy beings embody. This complex tapestry of beliefs and practices highlights Wicca's ongoing appeal as a spiritual path that celebrates diversity, harmony, and the great mysteries of existence.


## Polytheism and pantheism in Wicca

Wicca is a modern pagan religion with diverse beliefs derived from traditional and contemporary spirituality. The principles of pantheism and polytheism, which coexist and weave throughout the religion and provide a diverse perspective on the divine, are fundamental to Wiccan practice. Together, polytheism—the belief in several gods—and pantheism—the conviction that there is a divine presence in every part of the universe—create a comprehensive spiritual framework that reveres the individual gods and the holiness of the natural world.

The worship of numerous gods and goddesses from various cultural pantheons demonstrates Wicca's polytheism. Wiccans choose gods from mythologies such as Greek, Roman, Celtic, Norse, Egyptian, and others to respect, depending on which ones speak to their own experiences and beliefs. With this eclectic approach, practitioners can draw from a vast pool of mythical and symbolic images to create intimate relationships with the divine. A Wiccan, for example, would call upon the Celtic God Cernunnos, who represents the wild, untamed parts of nature, and the Greek goddess Artemis, who is associated with the moon and the wilderness. According to this polytheistic tradition, Wiccans can address different facets of life and nature with specific deities, each representing unique powers and principles.

Because the Wiccan pantheon is not strictly defined, it permits a flexible and all-encompassing conception of deity. The God and the Goddess, frequently regarded as archetypal representations of the male and female facets of the divine, are significant figures in Wiccan polytheism. The God, often portrayed as having horns, represents the sun, the natural world, and the life-death cycle. The goddess, sometimes called the Triple Goddess, embodies the moon and the Maiden, Mother, and Crone phases of womanhood. These gods are respected for their balancing roles in the cycles of human existence and the natural world, which offer a comprehensive framework for comprehending the cosmos.

Conversely, pantheism in Wicca represents the conviction that the divine is inherent in everything. According to this viewpoint, the entire cosmos expresses the sacred, with divinity permeating every aspect of the natural world. Wiccans emphasize the sacredness of the natural environment and the interconnection of all life by referring to this supernatural presence as the Great Spirit or the All. This pantheistic viewpoint fosters a profound respect for nature, which also promotes rituals that honor the land, the seasons, and life's cycles.

Wicca rituals and rites frequently incorporate elements of pantheism and polytheism, honoring both particular deities and the greater sanctity of the cosmos. For example, Wiccans may call upon specific seasonal gods and goddesses during a Sabbat, a seasonal festival, and celebrate the earth and the changing seasons as divine manifestations. By taking a dual approach, practitioners can develop a holistic spiritual practice by experiencing the sacred on a personal and universal level.

The practice of magic in Wicca also demonstrates the interaction between pantheism and polytheism. Wiccans hold that they can affect events and achieve their desires by connecting with the divine energy that permeates the universe. This kind of magick frequently entails calling upon certain gods for their unique qualities and abilities while acknowledging the innate divinity of every ceremony component. For example, a healing spell could acknowledge the sacred energy present in the ceremony's herbs and candles and call upon the goddess Brigid's healing powers.

Wicca offers a diverse and dynamic spiritual path because of its inclusive and flexible nature, enabling it to merge polytheism and pantheism easily. This integration reflects the Wiccan idea of the divine as both many and one, present in all aspects of the natural world but accessible through many forms. Wiccans interact with the various manifestations of the holy by honoring multiple deities, and pantheism guarantees that the sacred is acknowledged in everything, promoting a deep reverence for the natural world and all living creatures.

To sum up, pantheism and polytheism are pillars of Wiccan spirituality, offering contrasting frameworks for perceiving and connecting with the divine. While pantheism imbues the entire cosmos with sanctity, fostering a holistic and respectful approach to life, polytheism allows Wiccans to communicate with specific gods and goddesses, relying on their unique traits and powers. When combined, these ideas offer a spiritual path that respects the unity of all things and the plurality of the divine and is diverse, inclusive, and flexible. Through these two lenses, Wicca provides a profound and meaningful means to interact with the secrets of life, the natural world, and the universe.

# CHAPTER IV

# Sacred Texts and Symbols

## The Book of Shadows

Wicca is a contemporary paganism emphasizing nature worship, moon cycles, and respect for the God and Goddess. One of Wicca's primary and most essential components is the Book of Shadows. This book functions as a practitioner's grimoire, a compilation of spells, rites, invocations, and information to aid their spiritual development. The Book of Shadows' history, meaning, and composition provide profound insights into the customs and beliefs of the Wiccan tradition, characterized by diversity and change.

The genesis of contemporary Wicca, primarily attributed to Gerald Gardner, can be linked to the early 1900s and the Book of Shadows. Gardner, a vital role in the founding of Wicca, popularized the idea of the Book of Shadows as a storehouse of Wiccan teachings and magical knowledge. At first, Gardner's Book of Shadows drew extensively from various sources, such as folklore, ceremonial magic, and Aleister Crowley's works. With the addition of new publications by Gardner and his disciples over time, this collection of works changed to reflect the fluid and evolving character of Wiccan practice.

In Wiccan practice, a conventional Book of Shadows usually includes various material for various reasons. The collection of rituals is one of the main elements; rituals are necessary for magic and commemorating important events. Sabbats, which honor the Wiccan Wheel of the Year, and Esbats, full moon rites, are two examples of these rituals. To guarantee that these holy rituals are performed correctly, detailed instructions for performing ceremonies, calling on deities, and casting circles are frequently carefully documented. The Book of Shadows also includes spells and magical operations for various goals, including prosperity, love, healing, and protection. Typically, these spells are written in predetermined formats that specify the supplies needed, the exact procedures to be followed, and the incantations to be recited.

The Book of Shadows frequently includes invocations and petitions to gods, elements, spirits, rituals, and spells. Using these invocations, one might ask higher powers for direction, assistance, and blessings. Wiccans believe that the universe is permeated with divine powers, and they can show their appreciation and devotion to these forces through their prayers. These invocations emphasize the profoundly spiritual nature of Wiccan practice and the relationship between the practitioner and the sacred.

The presence of correspondences and symbolic linkages is a critical component of the Book of Shadows. Wiccans hold that certain hues, plants, stones, and symbols have their own energies and magical qualities. To increase the potency of rituals and spells, the Book of Shadows frequently includes thorough listings and explanations of these correspondences. For instance, an entry might discuss the protective and purifying qualities of rosemary or the meaning of the pentacle as a symbol of stability and the ground. For practitioners, these correspondences offer a valuable point of reference that helps them match their magical operations with the natural forces they are trying to channel.

One might also jot down personal thoughts, experiences, and revelations in the Book of Shadows. Many Wiccans keep journals to record the results of their rituals and spells, noting what worked, what didn't, and any lessons discovered. Through introspection and journaling, practitioners can improve their abilities, broaden their awareness, and create a more prosperous and individualized spiritual practice. The Book of Shadows develops into a personal relic, bearing witness to the practitioner's development and journey along the Wiccan path.

With the introduction of digital technology and the growing transparency of Wiccan practice, the Book of Shadows—formerly written by hand and kept confidential—has changed. Nowadays, some Wiccans keep digital copies of their Books of Shadows, organizing and storing their information on computers and other resources. This change illustrates Wicca's adaptable and modern nature, enabling practitioners to use modern tools in their age-old practices.

The Book of Shadows is a living text that changes with the practitioner; it is not merely a compendium of magical and spiritual wisdom. It represents the individual path of every Wiccan, showcasing their distinct encounters, realizations, and spiritual ties. The act of making and maintaining a Book of Shadows fosters a strong sense of engagement and dedication to the Wiccan path, which promotes ongoing study, introspection, and personal development.

To sum up, the Book of Shadows has a significant role in Wiccan practice. It is a thorough manual, a private diary, and a holy book that condenses the wisdom, spells, invocations, and rituals essential to the Wiccan way of life. Gerald Gardner's roots emphasize its historical relevance, and how its content has changed over time has highlighted how dynamic and individualized Wicca is. Whether preserved in its original handwritten form or updated for contemporary digital platforms, the Book of Shadows is still an essential resource for Wiccans, assisting them in their spiritual practices and providing a link to the timeless and ever-evolving currents of magical tradition.

## Key symbols (Pentacle, Triple Moon, etc.)

In Wiccan practice, symbols are fundamental because they serve as visual representations of the essential religion's ideas, energies, and principles. They symbolize spiritual identity, meditation aids, and ceremony focal points. The spiral, the ankh, the pentacle, and the triple moon are some of the most significant symbols in Wicca. Each of these symbols represents a different facet of Wiccan spirituality and is essential to the practice and comprehension of the faith.

In Wicca, the pentacle is arguably the most critical and well-known symbol. It is a pentagram, or five-pointed star, encircled by a circle. The pentagram's five primary elements—earth, air, fire, water, and spirit—are each represented by a different point. The circle that encircles the star represents harmony, safety, and life's cyclical nature. Invoking these elements and their corresponding energies through rituals and magical operations is a common usage of the pentacle. In addition, it is worn as an amulet for heavenly protection and direction. The Wiccan concept of interconnectedness is reflected in the symbol's emphasis on harmony and balance, emphasizing that all aspects of the universe are interconnected and should be revered.

The triple moon, which stands for the waxing, complete, and waning phases of the moon, is another important symbol in Wiccan lore. The Triple Goddess, who represents the Maiden, Mother, and Crone phases of a woman's existence, is likewise linked to this emblem. The waxing moon represents growth, fresh starts, and the youthful vitality of the maiden. The full moon symbolizes power, fulfillment, and the nurturing and creative qualities of the Mother. The waning moon represents the Crone's wisdom, reflection, and release. The triple moon symbol is frequently employed in ceremonies and meditations aimed at capturing the unique energy of every lunar stage. It reminds us of the phases of life and the cycles of nature, and it inspires Wiccans to respect and cooperate with these organic rhythms.

Wicca also honors the ankh, an ancient Egyptian emblem. A cross with a loop at the top stands for the unification of masculine and female forces and eternal life. The Wiccan concept of existence's cyclical nature resonates with the ankh's symbolism of life, death, and rebirth. It is frequently included in ceremonies emphasizing spiritual development, healing, and protection. The ankh's shape, similar to a key, represents its function as a key to spiritual understanding and excellent knowledge. Wicca's eclectic nature is shown by its assimilation into practice, which draws from many historic traditions to enhance its spiritual tapestry.

Another significant symbol in Wicca is the spiral, representing the soul's progression and life's journey. Spirals can be seen in many forms in nature, such as shells and the patterns found in galaxies. They represent how the universe is growing and changing throughout time. The spiral is a standard tool in Wiccan meditation and trance practices for connecting with the deeper currents of life and the cosmos. It stands for the external journey to establish a connection with the holy and the internal journey to self-discovery. The infinite loop of the spiral also represents eternity and the interdependence of all things.

In Wicca, the athame, a ceremonial knife, represents strength and purpose. It is used to cast circles and direct energy rather than cutting anything. Usually carrying a double-edged sword, the athame represents the duality of existence and the harmony of opposites. It stands for the force of the intellect and the element of air. The athame is used in ceremonies to delineate sacred territory and to call forth or drive out spiritual beings. The Wiccan concept that individuals may mold their world through concentrated purpose and magical practice is reinforced by the instrument's function as a tool of will and direction.

Because of its historical associations with the womb and the alchemical vessel, the cauldron symbolizes metamorphosis and rebirth. The cauldron is used in Wiccan ceremonies for divination (scrying), mixing potions, and burning offerings. It stands for both the goddess's transformational power and the water element. The image of the cauldron is associated with the legendary cauldrons of Celtic mythology, such as the Cauldron of Cerridwen, which bestows inspiration and knowledge. The Wiccan concepts of transformation, creation, and the never-ending cycle of birth, death, and rebirth are all embodied in this emblem.

In Wiccan tradition, the broom, also called the besom, symbolizes protection and cleansing. It is connected to the element of earth and harmony in the home. The broom has been traditionally used to clear negative energy and create sacred space. Moreover, it is a component of fertility and handfasting rites (Wiccan marriage ceremonies). Sweeping with the besom is a practical and symbolic exercise that symbolizes clearing both spiritual and physical places to make way for ritual practice.

Essential symbols in Wiccan practice include the pentacle, triple moon, ankh, spiral, athame, cauldron, and broom. These symbols provide Wiccans with a rich and meaningful framework for their spiritual journey by connecting them to the natural world, life cycles, and the supernatural powers they worship. They also serve as visual and ceremonial instruments that encapsulate the essential ideas and ideals of the faith. Wiccans strengthen their connection to the divine, improve their magical practices, and gain a deeper understanding of their faith by using and studying these symbols.

## Other influential texts and their significance

Wicca's beliefs, ceremonies, and practices, a modern pagan religious movement, are shaped by a wide range of books. Wiccan philosophy has been developed and disseminated through several important works, among which the Book of Shadows is arguably the most well-known and intimate among practitioners. Among the writings in this collection are "The Witch-Cult in Western Europe" by Margaret Murray, "The White Goddess" by Robert Graves, and pieces by Gerald Gardner and Doreen Valiente. Each book has made a distinctive contribution to our understanding of and practice in Wicca with its historical background, mythical insights, and helpful advice.

"The Witch-Cult in Western Europe," by Margaret Murray, released in 1921, is among the founding books that shaped Wicca's early evolution. Anthropologist Murray contended that the Early Modern period's witch trials targeted adherents of a still-existing pagan religion rather than being the product of persecution and panic. She proposed that this witch-cult was centered on fertility rites and worshipped a god with horns. Even though most modern historians reject Murray's beliefs, her writings significantly influenced Gerald Gardner and other early Wiccan pioneers. Her picture of a coherent, pre-Christian pagan religion gave Gardner and others a foundation for creating modern Wicca, validating it as a resurgence of pre-Christian religious rituals.

"The White Goddess," written by Robert Graves and initially published in 1948, is another essential work shaping Wiccan philosophy. The concept of a unique, strong goddess who is the moon's manifestation and the muse of poets is explored in Graves' book. By establishing links between different historical and mythological characters, he makes the case that widespread goddess worship was practiced in ancient Europe. Many Wiccans accepted the idea of the Goddess as a prominent character in their faith due to Graves' lovely and moving words. His focus on the Goddess's triple aspect as a maiden, mother, and crone resonates well with the ideas and rituals of Wicca, highlighting the significance of the feminine divine and the natural cycles.

Gerald Gardner, frequently called the "father of modern Wicca," was instrumental in popularizing Wicca through his works. His publications "The Meaning of Witchcraft" (1959) and "Witchcraft Today" (1954) are regarded as prerequisite reads for comprehending the tenets of Wiccan practice. In "Witchcraft Today," Gardner blends elements of ceremonial magic and folk traditions with the idea that Wicca continues the old witch cult, as Murray describes it. Wicca's structure and attractiveness were partly established by Gardner's depiction of it as a mystery religion with covens and secret rites. "The Meaning of Witchcraft" elaborates on these concepts, providing a more thorough explanation of Wiccan activities and beliefs. Gardner's writings served as a guide for generations of Wiccans, establishing the faith's organization, ethics, and rituals.

Often credited as the founder of contemporary Wicca, Doreen Valiente substantially impacted the practice of religion through her writings and partnership with Gardner. The Gardnerian rites that Valiente expanded and revised made the Wiccan practice more poetic and approachable. Her publications, including "Where Witchcraft Lives" (1962) and "An ABC of Witchcraft" (1973), are invaluable tools for practitioners of all skill levels. The spiritual depth of Wicca was enhanced by Valiente's emphasis on the lyrical and intuitive parts of the discipline and her inclusion of traditional folklore and magic. Her art emphasized how crucial it is to use creativity and personal experience to establish a connection with the holy and the natural world.

Another well-known member of the Wiccan community, Raymond Buckland, made a substantial contribution with his books and lectures. Buckland's 1974 book "The Tree: The Complete Book of Saxon Witchcraft" presented Seax-Wica, a Saxon paganism-based tradition he developed. His 1986 book "Buckland's Complete Book of Witchcraft" is widely known as the "Big Blue Book" and is an extensive resource for anyone curious about Wicca. This book is an invaluable resource for practitioners, covering various subjects, such as coven structure, divination, spells, and rituals. Buckland's practical and personable manner has contributed to demystifying Wicca and increasing its accessibility for a broader range of people.

Another important book that has influenced modern Wiccan and pagan ideas is Starhawk's "The Spiral Dance: A Rebirth of the Ancient Religion of the Great Goddess," published in 1979. In her writings, Starhawk highlights the feminist and eco-spiritual facets of Wicca and argues in favor of a spirituality that is closely linked to the natural cycles of the land. Her book offers a comprehensive approach to Wiccan practice by fusing theory, hands-on activities, and rituals. "The Spiral Dance" emphasizes the role of spirituality in promoting ecological awareness and social justice and has encouraged many people to investigate Wicca as a path of social and personal development.

In conclusion, a wide range of writings have greatly influenced the evolution of Wicca, each adding to the intricate web of rituals, practices, and beliefs that characterize the faith. The modern Wiccan movement has been influenced by a variety of works, including Margaret Murray's anthropological theories, Robert Graves' mythopoetic visions, Gerald Gardner's foundational writings, Doreen Valiente's poetic revisions, Raymond Buckland's helpful guides, and Starhawk's eco-feminist spirituality. They enable practitioners to connect with the ancient foundations of their faith while adjusting it to modern needs and insights by offering historical context, spiritual depth, and helpful guidance.

# CHAPTER V

# The Wheel of the Year

## Sabbats and their meanings

The eight festivals known as the Sabbats, commemorated in various paganism and earthly spiritual traditions, are significant for respecting the seasons and the year's rotation. Every Sabbat represents an essential moment in the seasonal cycle and has themes and symbolism that practitioners find particularly meaningful. Commencing on October 31 with Samhain, the Sabbats move through the following dates: Beltane, the summer solstice (Litha), Lammas (Lughnasadh), the autumn equinox (Mabon), the winter solstice (Yule), and Samhain once more.

The first Sabbat, Samhain, signifies the conclusion of the harvest season and the start of winter. It is a powerful time for remembering ancestors, contemplating death, and embracing change since it is thought to be the moment when the curtain between the realms of the living and the dead is thinnest. Yule, observed around December 21, commemorates the sun's return and the winter solstice, the year's longest night. It represents rebirth, the promise of fresh starts, and the victory of light over darkness.

Ostara is the spring equinox, a period when light and dark are in harmony, and it falls on or around March 21. It honors development, fertility, and the planet's waking from its winter hibernation. Celebrated on May 1, Beltane is a festival of life, passion, and fertility. It celebrates the marriage of the deity and goddess, represented by the life force of the natural world and flower blooming.

The summer solstice is the longest day of the year, which is observed on June 21, also known as Litha. It's a moment to rejoice in nature's bounty, the sun's zenith, and life itself. Harvest season begins with Lammas, sometimes called Lughnasadh, which falls on or around August 1. It's a moment to celebrate community, express gratitude for the land's abundance, and remember those who have given their lives to ensure our survival.

Mabon is a celebration of the second harvest and the autumn equinox that falls on or around September 21. It's a season of harmony, giving thanks, and getting ready for the gloomier half of the year. Every Sabbat has a distinct spirit and symbolism that reflects the natural world's cyclical dynamic of life, death, and rebirth. Practitioners develop a sense of reverence for the sacredness of life, strengthen their bond with the land, and respect the cycles of nature via rituals, ceremonies, and celebrations.

The Sabbaths remind us how intertwined we are with the entire web of life and how crucial it is to live in balance with the environment. They offer chances for introspection, spiritual development, and group celebration, encouraging a stronger sense of kinship with something bigger than us. We are urged to respect life's cycles, harmonize with the natural world's rhythms, and cherish each moment as we travel around the year's wheel.

## Celebrating the eight Sabbats

Observing the eight Sabbaths is a profoundly spiritual custom derived from earthly and pagan traditions. These Sabbats are called the Wheel of the Year, which charts a cyclical path through the seasons to help practitioners connect with the Earth's inherent rhythms. Starting on Samhain, the holy day that heralds the end of the harvest season and the coming of winter, the Sabbats continue with Yule. This winter solstice festival represents the return of light and continues with Ostara, the vernal equinox that represents rebirth and equilibrium. Beltane comes next, bringing themes of fertility, vigor, and the unification of divine spirits to announce the approach of spring. When the Wheel spins, Litha appears, commemorating the summer solstice when the sun is at its strongest. Lughnasadh, also known as Lammas, marks the beginning of the harvest season and the expression of thanksgiving for all that the Earth has to provide. Mabon, the autumnal equinox, celebrates the second harvest and the equilibrium between light and dark, bringing us full circle to Samhain.

Every Sabbath has a special meaning that provides a chance for spiritual introspection, interaction with nature, and a link to ancestor wisdom. Samhain, which falls on October 31, is a transitional period when it is said that the curtain between the world of spirits and the material world is the thinnest. This is a moment to pay tribute to the dead, accept your mortality, and celebrate the transformational power of death and rebirth. Celebrated around December 21, Yule represents hope, renewal, and the promise of light returning to the planet. It also symbolizes the longest night of the year and the sun's rebirth.

Ostara, usually celebrated on March 21, marks the beginning of spring and the equilibrium of day and night. This is a moment to rejoice in fresh starts, development, and the planet's waking from winter hibernation. The May 1st holiday, Beltane, is a joyful celebration of life, passion, and fertility. It's a moment to celebrate the holy marriage between the god and goddess, have fun, and dance around the maypole. Litha, which falls on June 21 and marks the summer solstice, represents the height of solar power and the profusion of life. It's a moment to celebrate the life of the planet, commune with nature, and soak up the sun's warmth.

The harvest season officially begins on August 1, with Lughnasadh, commonly called Lammas. It's a moment to celebrate communal sharing, express gratitude for the bounty of the Earth, and acknowledge the cycle of abundance and sacrifice. Mabon, which falls on September 21, symbolizes the second harvest and the autumnal equinox. It's a time to enjoy the fruits of our labor, give thanks for the year's gifts, and prepare for the dark and contemplative season ahead.

There are many different ways to celebrate the eight Sabbats: from solitary rituals to group get-togethers, from ornate ceremonies to straightforward acts of reverence in nature. Festivities, storytelling, crafts, meditation, and rituals honoring the elements and deities connected to each Sabbat are a few examples of activities that can occur. Utilizing these festivities, practitioners build gratitude, strengthen their bond with the planet, and synchronize themselves with natural cycles. The Sabbats are a great way to remember how interdependent all life is and how crucial it is to live in balance with the environment. They lead practitioners on a path of self-discovery and reconnection with life's sacred rhythms, providing chances for personal development, change, and spiritual renewal.

## Seasonal rites and customs

For thousands of years, seasonal rituals and customs have been integral to human societies, demonstrating the close bond between humans and the natural environment. These customs, rooted in the shifting of the seasons, signify changes, commemorate plenty, and respect life's cycles. Diverse customs have arisen across countries and nations, each with a unique meaning and symbolism connected to the natural cycles.

Seasonal change is especially significant in many agricultural communities—for instance, the arrival of spring signals the earth's awakening from its winter hibernation. The return of light and warmth is celebrated on old holidays like the Hindu Holi and the Celtic Imbolc, which stand for fertility, fresh starts, and the victory of life over death. To get people and communities ready for the rebirth of life, these ceremonies frequently include purifying rituals like cleaning fires or symbolic bathing.

The summer solstice signifies the zenith of light and energy as the year revolves around. Celebrations honoring the sun's strength and richness in nature occur on this day across cultures. While contemporary Wiccans and adherents of other earthly spiritualities celebrate Litha, a season of joy, development, and celebration of the vitality of the natural world, the ancient Greeks observed the festival of Kronia, which was dedicated to the agricultural deity Cronus. Typical midsummer celebrations include bonfires, feasting, and dancing, which promote a sense of community and a connection to the earth's cycles.

Communities prepare for the harvest, and the approach of winter with a unique collection of rituals and customs observed in the fall. Lammas, or Lughnasadh, is a Celtic festival that honors the first fruits of the crop and the god Lugh. It is a season of giving thanks, celebrating the bounty of labor and the interdependence of all living things, and getting together as a community. Similarly, the Japanese custom of Tsukimi, or moon-viewing, honors the beauty of the harvest season and the fall moon. Rice dumpling offerings and seasonal reflection frequently mark it.

Last but not least, the winter solstice is the longest night of the year, a period of reflection and gloom tinged with the hope of light returning. Around the globe, societies commemorate this occasion with rites of rebirth, hope, and regeneration. The festival of Saturnalia, a week of eating, gift-giving, and celebration, was how the ancient Romans paid homage to Saturn, the god of agriculture. In the meantime, Yule, a Norse holiday, marked the return of the sun and the prospect of longer days ahead. Ceremonies frequently featured feasts, storytelling by the hearth, and evergreen tree planting.

Seasonal rituals and customs have shaped human experience throughout history and geography, giving people a feeling of continuity, community, and connection to the natural world. These customs serve as a reminder of our place in the chain of life and the significance of protecting and caring for the planet at a time when people are becoming more and more cut off from the cycles of the natural world. Seasonal rituals give our life meaning and purpose by providing opportunities for introspection, celebration, and reconnecting, whether derived from traditional festivals or contemporary adaptations.

# CHAPTER VI

# Esbats and Lunar Magic

## The significance of the moon phases

For thousands of years, people have been captivated by the moon's ethereal beauty and its enormous impact on the Earth and its inhabitants. From the new moon to the full moon and back, the moon's phases are fundamental to many facets of scientific understanding, natural phenomena, and human culture. These phases are more than just a celestial display; they are essential to the natural world and human society. They are caused by the moon's orbit around Earth and the relative locations of the moon, Earth, and sun.

One of its most important features is the moon phases' impact on the tides. The moon's and the sun's gravitational pull on Earth's seas cause the tides, which are a regular rise and decrease in sea levels. The sun, moon and Earth align during the new and complete moon phases, causing spring tides characterized by higher high tides and lower low tides. On the other hand, neap tides, characterized by less drastic tidal shifts, happen during the first and third quarters of the moon, when the sun and moon are at right angles to the Earth. Many marine organisms' behavior and life cycles are influenced by these tidal motions, which are essential to coastal ecosystems. They also significantly impact human endeavors, including fishing, coastal management, and navigation.

The moon's phases have been given symbolic connotations in human culture and are integral to many customs and calendars. Numerous ancient civilizations created lunar calendars, such as the Greeks, Egyptians, and Chinese, based on the moon's cycles. These calendars controlled social gatherings, religious holidays, and agricultural activity. For example, based on the moon's cycles, the Islamic calendar establishes the dates of significant religious holidays like Eid and Ramadan. The dates of traditional celebrations like the Lunar New Year and the Mid-Autumn Festival are determined by the Chinese calendar, which also considers solar and lunar cycles. The moon's phases have also impacted mythology, literature, and the arts; they frequently represent transition, change, and the passage of time.

For astronomical and scientific investigations, the moon's phases are also crucial. Astronomers can learn facts about the moon's orbit and the mechanics of the Earth, moon, and sun system by monitoring the moon's phases. The topography and composition of the lunar surface can be inferred from the shifting angles at which sunlight reflects off the surface over the moon's many phases. For instance, the full moon, which occurs when the moon is entirely illuminated by the sun, makes it possible to examine lunar features like craters and maria, which are broad, dark plains, in great detail. These observations have greatly aided our knowledge of the moon's origin and geological past.

Furthermore, the moon's phases have useful ramifications for space exploration. Planning lunar missions requires understanding how the moon's phases affect the lighting conditions on its surface. NASA meticulously planned landings during the Apollo missions to provide ideal lighting conditions for the astronauts, striking a balance between enough light and comfortable temperatures. Moon phase knowledge is still used to direct modern lunar missions, as engineers and scientists create rovers and other machinery that can survive the harsh lunar environment.

Moon phase relevance also goes into the domain of biological rhythms. Numerous terrestrial and marine organisms display physiological changes and behaviors corresponding to the lunar cycle. To provide the most excellent conditions for the survival of their progeny, several marine animals, like coral and some kinds of fish, schedule their spawning events to coincide with specific moon phases. The moonlight available to nocturnal animals—such as certain birds and mammals—affects their activity, impacting their foraging and predator avoidance tactics.

The moon's phases have long been utilized in agriculture to direct planting and harvesting procedures. Some people still engage in the ancient practice of lunar gardening, which is predicated on the idea that the moon's gravitational pull influences plant growth and soil moisture. Crops that grow above ground during the waxing moon (from new moon to full moon) and below ground during the waning moon (from full moon to new moon) are recommended for planting, according to proponents of this strategy. Despite the lack of scientific backing, these rituals demonstrate a long-standing relationship between agriculture, human activity, and the lunar cycle.

In summary, the moon's phases are more than just a celestial occurrence; they are intricately entwined with the natural world's cycles and human civilization. The moon's phases have a wide range of effects, from affecting animal behavior and ocean tides to impacting scientific research and cultural customs. Indeed, the moon's phases will remain a source of astonishment and a key to solving the mysteries of our cosmos as we continue to explore and comprehend our lunar friend.

## Rituals for Esbats

Wiccans and other neopagan practitioners commemorate the phases of the moon, especially the full moon, with esbats, which are rituals or get-togethers. Esbats are lunar festivities that happen thirteen times a year, by the full moon, in contrast to the more popular Sabbats connected to the solar cycle and the changing seasons. These events are deeply spiritually significant because they allow practitioners to worship the Goddess, frequently linked to the moon in Wiccan tradition, and connect with the lunar energies.

Because the full moon is thought to be a time of increased power and energy, it is a perfect time to practice witchcraft and other spiritual pursuits. It is believed that the light of a full moon brings clarity and understanding to both the physical and spiritual realms. Because of this, Esbat rituals are frequently focused on tasks like spellcasting, divination, and healing that call for increased magickal potency. To maximize the effectiveness of their workings under the full moon's glow, practitioners can ensure that they are ready in advance by setting their intentions and gathering the required equipment and materials.

Usually, an Esbat ceremony starts with the establishment of a sacred area. To consecrate the place, practitioners can draw a circle around the ritual location and invoke the elements of fire, water, air, and earth. Circle casting is an essential part of the Wiccan ritual, acting as a barrier between the material and spiritual worlds and shielding those inside from evil energy. In addition, the circle represents fullness and oneness, mirroring the moon's cyclical cycle and the interdependence of all things.

Following the casting of the circle, practitioners frequently invoke God and the Goddess, the two primary deities in Wiccan doctrine. As the moon's Maiden, Mother, and Crone phases, which stand for the various stages of life and facets of feminine energy, the Goddess is commonly connected to the moon. Despite being frequently linked to the sun, God is also recognized during Esbats, highlighting the harmony between masculine and feminine energies. The ceremony is initiated with prayers or invocations to these deities, asking for their assistance and presence.

One of the main elements of an esbat is the Drawing Down the Moon ceremony, in which the High Priestess or another practitioner transfers the Goddess' energy into oneself. This profoundly transformational and intensely meditative practice allows one to embody the divine and obtain profound insights. It is thought that the practitioner gains strength from the moon's energy, which improves their capacity for magickal operations and spiritual communication.

After the Drawing Down the Moon, practitioners can do whatever magick they like. During Esbats, spellcasting is a popular activity. Spells are frequently directed toward objectives like love, prosperity, protection, and personal development. These spells are considered especially powerful because of the full moon's energy, which is believed to magnify the intentions set forth. Furthermore, many people use divination techniques like scrying, rune casting, and tarot reading to get insight and assistance on significant issues. It is said that the intense moonlight improves psychic powers and facilitates access to hidden knowledge.

The full moon's lighting and nourishing powers are said to help with physical, mental, and spiritual healing; thus, healing rites are also prevalent during Esbats. Practitioners can carry out rituals to balance and purify their energies, let go of negativity, and advance general well-being. Utilizing the qualities of crystals, herbs, and other natural materials in combination with lunar energy, these healing rituals frequently incorporate these aspects.

Esbats offer a chance for celebration, community building, and magical operations. In communal environments, practitioners might partake in food and beverages, frequently through a symbolic "cakes and ale" ceremony, stabilizing the energy generated throughout the ritual and promoting a feeling of belonging. This community element plays a key role in strengthening the bonds between practitioners and fostering an atmosphere conducive to spiritual development.

The ceremony ends with the closing of the circle and the expression of gratitude to the deities and elemental forces for their support and presence. With this deed, sacred time and space end, enabling practitioners to return to their regular lives with the benefits and wisdom of the Esbat.

Esbats are elaborate, multidimensional ceremonies that respect the lunar cycles and utilize their energy for magical and spiritual ends. They frequently give practitioners a chance to celebrate the cycles of nature, work toward personal goals, and strengthen their connection with the divine. Wiccans and other neopagans sustain lively and dynamic contact with the moon forces that have enthralled humanity since the beginning of time through the customs and rituals connected with Esbats.


## Moon magic and its applications

Moon magic is a profound and age-old discipline that uses a variety of rituals and spells to harness the moon's energy. It is based on the moon's natural cycles. A fundamental component of many witchcraft and neopaganism traditions, this type of magic is intricately linked to the moon's phases. It reflects the moon's power over the planet and its people. Moon magic has many applications that affect personal development, spiritual understanding, and physical health, among other areas of life.

Knowing the energies associated with each moon phase is essential to moon magic. The new moon, waxing crescent, first quarter, waxing gibbous, full moon, waning gibbous, last quarter, and waning crescent are all part of the lunar cycle, lasting about 29.5 days. Every phase has unique properties and can be used for various magical operations. For instance, the new moon symbolizes beginnings and is a great time to make resolutions, begin new endeavors, and channel new energy. As the moon approaches fullness, the waxing phase is a period of development, attraction, and construction. It works exceptionally well for spells that increase riches, strengthen personal power, and improve health.

The full moon, the apex of the lunar cycle, is said to be the most potent time to perform magical work. Its energy is thought to magnify the strength of spells, making it the best time to carry out protection rituals, perform divination, and actualize desires. The full moon's light is believed to give clarity and insight, illuminating the mind and spirit. This stage is also linked to fulfillment and completion, so it's a good time to finish work and recognize successes.

The energy of the waning moon, which occurs when it goes from complete to new, is said to be favorable to release, banishing, and contemplation. The waning moon is an auspicious time to perform purification rituals, remove barriers, and give up bad habits. This stage encourages self-reflection and introspection, enabling practitioners to evaluate their development, draw lessons from their mistakes, and prepare for the following cycle.

Moon magic is used extensively in spellcasting when practitioners synchronize their objectives with the moon's phases to maximize its efficacy. For example, charms for development and attraction, like drawing prosperity or love, are cast during the waxing moon. Candles, crystals, herbs, and other symbolic objects that align with the practitioner's intentions may be used in these spells. On the other hand, spells known as banishing are performed under the waning moon to eliminate negativity or break undesirable habits. These spells frequently use black candles, salt, and protective symbols.

Moon magic is also often used in divination, the art of using supernatural methods to get knowledge. Because of its connection to light and clarity, the full moon is especially preferred for divination techniques like rune casting, scrying, and tarot reading. The full moon's light is said to improve psychic powers and offer more discernible insights. Many practitioners also deal with dreams during this period, using lucid dreaming and astral travel to extract messages and advice.

Moon magic is also essential to healing techniques. The moon's phases are thought to influence the body's innate rhythms and tides. Healing rituals frequently correspond with particular lunar phases to meet the body's needs. For instance, rituals targeted at both physical and emotional well-being are most effective during the waxing moon, which is thought to be beneficial for healing and regeneration. Conversely, the waning moon is a time for clearing the body of impurities and letting go of emotional or physical burdens.

Moon magic has practical uses and is essential to many spiritual traditions and group ceremonies. For Wiccans and other neopagans, esbats, or monthly celebrations of the full moon, are important events. These customs promote community and spiritual connection, frequently including group meditations, potluck dinners, and group spellcasting. The full moon's energy is harnessed to increase the effectiveness of the ceremonies and fortify the ties between participants.

Moreover, there is a strong connection between moon magic and the cycles of nature. Practitioners widely use Moon magic to connect with the earth's cycles and shifting seasons. The moon's phases arrange planting, harvesting, and other agricultural tasks in a custom known as "gardening by the moon," which maximizes growth and productivity. Living in balance with the natural world and its cycles is a larger philosophy reflected in this practice.

Moon magic is, at its core, a diverse art that uses the moon's phases to affect several facets of life. Its enormous power and variety are demonstrated by its applications in healing, divination, spellcasting, and social rituals. Moon magic practitioners aim to harness the lunar energy by aligning with the lunar cycle, which promotes spiritual insight, personal progress, and a stronger bond with the natural world. This age-old method is still popular because it provides a timeless empowerment and personal growth route.

# CHAPTER VII

# Tools and Altars

## Common Wiccan tools (Athame, Chalice, Wand, etc.)

Tools are essential in Wiccan practice since they support ritualistic actions and represent more profound spiritual meanings. They are used to direct intents, focus energy, and establish a connection with the divine. Each has unique functions and symbolic meanings. The athame, chalice, wand, pentacle, and cauldron are some of the most often used Wiccan implements; each is essential to various rites and ceremonies.

In Wicca, one of the most recognizable objects is the athame, a double-edged ritual knife. Its main uses are invoking deities or elemental spirits, casting circles, and directing energy. Since the athame's blade is meant for symbolic actions of severing or pulling energy rather than actual cutting, it is typically not very sharp. The athame, which is traditionally connected to either the element of fire or air, stands for willpower and the principle of activity that is dynamic and male. The athame is used in ceremonies to consecrate other ritual objects, guide energy flow, and draw magical symbols. Its application emphasizes how crucial intent and concentration are to Wiccan witchcraft.

The chalice, a cup or goblet that contains fluids during rituals (typically water or wine), complements the athame. The chalice represents the feminine principle, frequently connected to the Goddess and water element. It stands for intuition, openness, and the caring quality of the divine. The chalice is used in ritual practices to make offerings, make libations, and share the drink symbolically among participants, which promotes a sense of connection and community. During the Great Rite, the athame is dipped into the chalice to represent the balance and harmony in nature, signifying the merging of masculine and feminine elements.

Another crucial instrument in Wiccan rituals is the wand, frequently constructed of metal, crystal, or wood. Like the athame, it is an energy-directing instrument for a more adaptable and versatile use. The wand symbolizes the practitioner's will and will and is connected to the fire or air element. It is employed to draw symbols in the air or on surfaces, call forth gods, and cast circles. The practitioner's preferences and the particular magical properties they wish to utilize can influence the wand's choice of wood or material. Using the wand emphasizes the practitioner's bond with the elements and the natural world.

A potent symbol in Wicca, the pentacle is usually a flat disc with a five-pointed star inside a circle engraved on it. It symbolizes the earth element and stands for stability, protection, and grounding. The pentacle is used to sanctify other items and ritual locations and is frequently put on the altar as a focal point for ceremonies. The five elements—earth, air, fire, water, and spirit—that each end of the star represents represent the interdependence of all things. The circle that encircles the star represents life's cycle and harmony. Using the pentacle in ceremonies highlights the holistic aspect of Wiccan thought, combining all components into a unified spiritual practice.

In Wiccan tradition, the cauldron is a multipurpose and symbolic item typically connected to the Goddess and the water element. It stands for metamorphosis, rebirth, and the enigmas of the divine feminine. Traditionally associated with the legendary pots of Celtic mythology, it serves as a vessel for ceremonial fires and is used in ceremonies for concoction preparation, scrying, and incense burning. The cauldron's womb-like shape emphasizes its connection to creation and rebirth. The cauldron is used in rituals as a vessel for transformation, where ingredients are combined and altered to represent the practitioner's spiritual journey and the natural alchemical processes.

Wiccans employ additional objects in addition to these main tools to improve their ceremonies and daily practices. Invoking deities, setting intentions, and establishing holy spaces are all done with candles, which represent fire and illumination elements. Burning incense, connected to the element of air, cleanses the ritual space, elevates the energy, and conveys prayers to the almighty. Because of their unique energetic qualities, crystals and stones are used in meditation, healing, and protection. Herbs have specific magical correspondences and are utilized in teas, incense mixtures, and spells.

In Wiccan ceremonies, every tool—the athame, chalice, wand, pentacle, or cauldron, for example—has a specific and essential function. They are channels for heavenly energy and not just objects but extensions of the practitioner's desire. Wiccans' love for the natural environment and their spiritual practice is reflected in the thoughtful selection and consecration of these tools. Through these instruments, practitioners strengthen their contact with the divine forces that direct their lives, connect with old traditions, and harmonize with natural cycles. Wiccans engage in a dynamic, transforming practice that celebrates the seen and unseen parts of existence through ritual and the thoughtful use of these sacred artifacts.

## Setting up an altar

In many religious and spiritual traditions, such as Wicca, paganism, and other modern forms of witchcraft, setting up an altar is a very personal and spiritual practice that serves as the center for rituals, meditation, and daily devotional activities. An altar offers a hallowed area where people can concentrate their intents and energies, respect deities, ancestors, and nature spirits, and establish a spiritual connection with the divine. Making an altar is a personal procedure reflecting the practitioner's values, goals, and aesthetic tastes. This section examines the essential elements of erecting an altar, such as picking a site, organizing equipment and symbols, and caring for the sacred area.

Selecting an excellent place to build an altar is the first stage in the process. The site needs to be somewhere one is at ease and where there won't be any disturbances to the altar. It might be a simple setup to put together and take down, or it can be a permanent fixture in a particular space. An altar is often placed in a bedroom, living room, or a specific spiritual space. To establish a direct connection with the elements and the natural world, outdoor altars can also be made in gardens or other natural areas. The chosen space should be tidy, serene, and suitable for concentrated spiritual practice.

When a place has been chosen, the surface that will act as the altar needs to be prepared. A table, shelf, or other flat surface that can accommodate multiple items could be used for this. The surface has to be cleansed and blessed frequently with an elemental ceremony. For example, one could cleanse the area with sage or incense, add light and positivity with a candle, and purify the area with salt water. This preparation method establishes the altar's purpose and creates a sacred atmosphere.

The instruments and symbols set on the altar are in the center. These elements can differ significantly depending on the practitioner's preferences and tradition. For example, a pentacle or stone for earth, a censer or incense for air, a candle or wand for fire, and a chalice or bowl of water are typical components of a Wiccan altar.

These objects stand for the interdependence of all things and the harmony of natural forces. The altar's surface is usually covered with an altar cloth, which adds a layer of symbolic meaning and visual appeal. The altar cloth is generally chosen to match the season, rite, or god being worshiped.

An altar frequently has holy symbols in addition to representations of the elements. To respect and call upon the presence of deities, ancestors, or spirit guides, statues or images of them are frequently positioned on the altar. By acting as focal points during meditation and prayer, these symbols support practitioners in connecting with the spiritual energy they stand for. As expressions of thanks and devotion, offerings are also made on the altar, including food, flowers, and libations. Candles are commonly used to symbolize the transformation of energy and the light of the divine. Candle colors might be selected according to the practitioner's aims or magical correspondences.

Essential elements of the altar also include instruments and personal things that are particularly meaningful to the practitioner. These might be anything that connects with the practitioner's spiritual path, such as feathers, shells, talismans, crystals, or anything else. Every object on the altar should be arranged harmoniously, reflecting the practitioner's inner landscape and spiritual objectives by placing them all with intention. Items can be arranged according to ritual requirements, customary correspondences, or gut feeling.

An altar requires constant upkeep, which includes cleaning it often, replenishing offerings, and occasionally switching out the things to correspond with the passing of the moon, the seasons, or individual spiritual cycles. This maintenance keeps the altar in harmony with the practitioner's developing practice and keeps it energetically active. To maintain a strong spiritual connection and keep the altar's energy active, many practitioners have daily or weekly rituals at their altars, including lighting candles, reciting prayers, or engaging in meditation.

Additionally, an altar can be a dynamic place that adapts to the practitioner's requirements and annual cycles. To honor the ground's shifting energies, seasonal decorations can be added, such as flowers in the spring, fruits and grains in the fall, or evergreen branches in the winter. For specific rituals, like those honoring the Sabbats, Esbats, or personal anniversaries, special altars can be set up, each customized to the event's unique energies and intentions.

To sum up, creating an altar is a very intimate and significant rite that forms the basis of ritual and spiritual endeavors. The process includes selecting a good place, setting up the area, and carefully positioning instruments and symbols that align with the practitioner's goals and beliefs. The altar can be kept energetically lively and indicative of the practitioner's spiritual journey by providing frequent upkeep and seasonal modifications. By building and maintaining an altar, practitioners create a sacred area that strengthens their spiritual practice, opens doors to divine communication, and continuously reminds them of their spiritual journey.

## Sacred spaces and their maintenance

In many spiritual traditions, sacred spaces are important places for prayer, meditation, and spiritual connection. Whether they are natural locations, churches, temples, or personal altars, these places represent the sacredness of the universe and the divine and act as centers of spiritual activity. Establishing and preserving hallowed areas is crucial to cultivating a favorable atmosphere for spiritual development, introspection, and group devotion. This section examines the characteristics of sacred places, their significance, and the rituals necessary to preserve their holiness.

Sacred places are present in many religious traditions and cultures, and they each reflect the rituals and beliefs of their followers in a different way. Churches and cathedrals are holy places in Christianity, where devotees congregate for prayer and worship. Hinduism is home to many temples, all devoted to different gods and created to allow for direct communication with the divine. Mosques are places of worship and gathering places for Muslims. Natural places like mountains, rivers, and trees are revered by many indigenous societies as sacred places that represent the spirits of the land and ancestors. Personal altars and ritual areas are created in Wicca and modern Pagan religions to pay homage to the elements, spirits, and gods.

Deliberate and significant steps are needed to establish a sacred space—a location set aside for spiritual pursuits. This approach usually starts with picking a calm, motivating, and contemplative place. For many people, this could be a peaceful area in a house, a private garden, or a naturally occurring location in the outdoors. After being selected, the area is usually cleared of sluggish or negative energy after being selected. There are several ways to carry out this cleansing, including smudging with sage or other holy plants, sprinkling salt or holy water, or clearing the energy using sound therapy like chanting or ringing bells.

The actual arrangement of a sacred space frequently involves placing objects, utensils, and symbols that have spiritual meaning. Candles, crystals, religious literature, sculptures of deities, and natural items like flowers, stones, or feathers can all be found on personal altars. Every object is arranged thoughtfully to create a space that mirrors the practitioner's spiritual activities and values. Similar care is taken to decorate and arrange more significant community sacred buildings, like churches or temples, to honor the divine and promote worship.

Sacred space maintenance is a continuous process that calls for spiritual and physical upkeep. In terms of appearance, this entails maintaining the area tidy, ordered, and beautiful. It is customary to sweep, clean, and replenish offerings regularly. This could entail caring for the garden, removing trash, and ensuring the environment is respected and conserved for outside sacred locations. Maintaining the physical aspects of a holy place is considered an act of devotion that shows one's respect and reverence for the divine rather than merely a work.

Maintaining a sacred area spiritually calls for regular rituals and actions that uphold and perpetuate its purity. Regular prayers, meditations, and offerings made at the altar or in the sacred area can all fall under this category. Many traditions involve regular rituals to re-consecrate the space, guaranteeing that it is a powerful and holy place. This could entail re-purifying the space using smoke, water, or sound and restating the original aims and purpose of the location.

In communal sacred locations, community effort is frequently required for maintenance. Cleaning, decorating, and setting up the area for events and worship sessions may fall to volunteers or appointed caretakers. Involving the community in maintaining the sacred regions guarantees their preservation and fortifies ties between participants, encouraging a sense of commitment and shared responsibility.

Sacred places are essential for reasons other than only their physical and spiritual maintenance. They provide refuge for introspection, recovery, and metamorphosis. People can withdraw from the tensions and diversions of daily life in these areas, finding comfort and tranquility in their relationship with God. Sacred locations are Crucial to commemorate life's important events; seasonal celebrations, marriages, funerals, and births are frequently held there, giving them a more profound significance and meaning.

Furthermore, sacred places are necessary for group worship and the development of a shared spiritual identity. They offer a place where people can gather to partake in rites, ceremonies, and lessons, strengthening ties to the community and ideals they share. This communal feature of sacred places emphasizes how important it is for them to preserve and transmit cultural and religious traditions from generation to generation.

In summary, sacred places are essential for spiritual practice since they provide havens for solitary introspection and group prayer. While their upkeep necessitates continuous physical and spiritual care, their construction entails deliberate acts to identify and consecrate spaces for spiritual activities. These areas serve as refuges for introspection and metamorphosis, commemorating momentous occasions and building a shared identity. By creating and maintaining sacred spaces with reverence, practitioners uphold their spiritual traditions and pay homage to the divine, guaranteeing their continuous relevance and vitality in the contemporary world.

# CHAPTER VIII

# Spell craft and Magic

## The basics of spellcasting

Magic and spellcraft are age-old traditions based on the idea that people can affect the natural world by directing energy and setting intentions. Spellcasting, essential to many spiritual and esoteric traditions, is the practice of changing one's surroundings or circumstances via symbolic actions, spoken words, and particular equipment. Knowing the fundamentals of spellcasting necessitates an understanding of the elements that make up a spell and the moral issues that surround it.

The idea of energy lies at the core of spellcasting. Practitioners hold that energy makes up everything in the universe, including feelings and ideas. One can direct and focus this energy to produce desired results. This view is linked to the concept of intention, which is the spell's objective or purpose. It is essential to have a clear and concentrated goal because it is what attracts the energy needed to bring about the desired outcome. A protection spell, for example, would be based on a strong desire to protect oneself or someone from danger.

Spellcasting usually starts with preparation, which includes focusing the mind, selecting a suitable time and place, and assembling the required equipment. Because some spells are thought to work better at certain times of the month or on particular days of the week, timing can be crucial. For instance, a full moon is considered potent for spells needing extra energy, and a new moon is frequently associated with fresh starts. The practitioner should be able to focus without distractions in a peaceful, calm environment. This area is commonly cleansed and sanctified to create a favorable atmosphere for the spell to eliminate any bad or sluggish energy.

While many different tools and materials are used in spellcasting, some common ones are candles, crystals, herbs, and written symbols, often known as sigils. Every tool has unique energy qualities and symbolic connotations. For example, candles are commonly utilized because they symbolize both the transformational power of light and the element of fire. The candle's color is selected according to its correspondences: red is for love, green is for prosperity, and so forth. Rose quartz is linked to love and healing, while sage is recognized for its purifying properties. Crystals and herbs are chosen based on their purported magical properties. Sigils are symbols made to stand for specific intentions; they are frequently carved or drawn to serve as centers of energy for spells.

The practitioner usually casts a circle after setting up the area and gathering the necessary materials. This is a symbolic act of establishing a holy area that separates the material world from the spiritual domain. The circle has two purposes: it holds the energy created during the spell and shields the practitioner from outside threats. The elements—earth, air, fire, and water—are typically invoked before the circle is cast, and occasionally, a plea for direction or support from gods, spirits, or ancestors is made as well.

The practitioner then casts the circle and executes the spell. This can entail several techniques, including using tools and materials in particular ways, chanting or reciting incantations, lighting candles, and picturing the intended result. The practitioner must be able to see the goal clearly in their mind's eye and have the sensation that it has already been accomplished, which makes visualization an essential element. This facilitates more efficient energy direction and intention focus.

The practitioner closes the circle after casting the spell, releasing the elemental forces, and thanking any summoned spirits. The instruments are frequently cleaned and put away, and any materials left over, such as candle stubs or herbs, are burned or buried in a way that honors the environment. This last phase guarantees that the sacred area is restored to its original state and that the spell's energy is appropriately grounded.

In spellcraft, ethical considerations are critical. The Wiccan Rede, which says, "An it harm none, do what ye will," is followed by many practitioners. This idea emphasizes that one should refrain from hurting others or interfering with their free choice to promote ethical spellcasting. Another widely held belief is the law of threefold return, which states that any positive or negative energy that a person sends out into the world will return to them threefold. These moral precepts aid in guaranteeing that spellcasting is applied positively and helpfully.

To sum up, spellcraft and magic are intricate arts that combine ritual, symbolism, and purpose to harness and direct energy for desired results. The fundamentals of spellcasting are preparation, the use of symbolic tools, casting a circle, performing the spell, and ethical concerns to ensure responsible practice. By grasping these fundamental components, practitioners can effectively engage in spellcraft and use it as a tool for personal growth, healing, and positive change in their lives and the world around them.

## Types of spells and their purposes

A key component of magical practice is the employment of spells and tools for directing and capturing energy for specific purposes. They are ritualistically and intentionally created, using ingredients, symbols, and individual strength to achieve the desired results. Based on their intended uses—such as protection, love, healing, prosperity, and banishing—spells can be divided into several categories. Every kind of spell has a distinct purpose and uses particular tools and techniques to accomplish its objectives.

One of the most popular spells is protection, which is cast to keep people, places, or things safe from harm or bad energy. The protective barrier repels unwanted energies and creatures that these spells generate. There are several ways to cast protection spells, including making salt circles, calling upon guardian spirits or deities, or protecting amulets. Common implements are herbs like sage and rosemary, which have purifying qualities, and black candles, which are thought to absorb negativity. Another common approach is visualization, in which the practitioner imagines themselves or their home surrounded by a light barrier. Protection spells are mainly used to keep people safe and secure in their surroundings.

Love spells can improve relationships, draw in love, or promote acceptance and self-love. Rose petals, red or pink candles, rose quartz crystals, and other objects linked to love and attraction are frequently used in these rituals. Speaking incantations and affirmations strengthens the goal of attracting love into one's life. It is essential to approach love spells ethically to make sure they respect other people's right to free will. Love spells can promote confidence and self-love, strengthen the bonds in a current relationship, or draw in a new loving partner.

Promoting mental, emotional, and spiritual well-being is the primary goal of healing spells. They promote general health and harmony, aid in the healing process following illness, and ease pain. Natural ingredients with restorative qualities, such as herbs like lavender and chamomile, which have relaxing effects, and gems like amethyst, which are linked to emotional healing, are frequently included in healing spells. Using visualization techniques, practitioners can transmit healing energy to the injured area or individual. These spells are meant to promote and enhance the body's natural healing processes and are intended to be used in addition to medical care.

Spells for prosperity are meant to draw success, money, and plenty. Opportunities for monetary gain, professional growth, and general prosperity can be unlocked using these spells. They frequently use gold or green candles, money symbols like cash or banknotes, and abundance-associated spices like cinnamon and basil. The practitioner's intention to attract prosperity is focused on affirmations and images. Creating charm bags full of money-attracting objects or carrying out rituals at auspicious astrological seasons are other examples of prosperity spells. Prosperity spells aim to assist practitioners in achieving their career and financial goals by directing their energy toward the flow of abundance in the universe.

Spells for banishing are used to get rid of undesirable influences, energies, or habits from a person's life. By cleansing and purifying, these spells pave the path for constructive transformation and development. Spells for banishing can be used to rid oneself of harmful thoughts, break unhealthy habits, and remove oneself from poisonous situations or relationships. Black candles and purifying plants like garlic and sage are standard instruments that symbolize the eradication of negativity. In rituals, the practitioner could write down things they want to eliminate and then burn the paper to represent that release. Banishing spells aim to remove barriers and make room for fresh starts.

Spells of divination are employed for guidance and insight but are not intended to bring about change. Tarot cards, runes, and scrying mirrors are standard instruments used in these spells, which enable practitioners to access their intuition and the wisdom of the cosmos. Spells of divination can illuminate obscure information, facilitate decision-making, and provide a peek at what lies ahead. They are carried out to comprehend more general life patterns or find answers to particular concerns.

To sum up, spells can be divided into many kinds according to what they are meant to achieve, such as divination, healing, prosperity, protection, love, or banishment. Every type of magic uses particular techniques, ingredients, and intents to accomplish its objectives. Spells for protection build walls against negativity; spells for love draw and strengthen relationships; spells for healing promote mental and physical health; spells for prosperity draw money and success; spells for banishing pull out bad influences; and spells for divination seek wisdom and direction. Practitioners can effectively use the power of magic to better their lives and align with their most profound objectives by understanding these types of spells and their purposes.

## Ethical considerations in spell work

In spell work, ethical issues are crucial because they direct practitioners toward using their magical skills honorably and responsibly. The art of spellcasting, which is based chiefly on the manipulation of intention and energy, can significantly impact the practitioner, those around them, and other people. Practitioners must follow ethical guidelines that put damage minimization, respect for human free will, and compatibility with universal values first.

The Wiccan Rede, summed up in words, "An it harm none, do what ye will," is one of the foremost moral precepts of spellcraft. This principle highlights the significance of thinking through the possible outcomes of one's activities and preventing harm to the environment, others, and oneself. It is recommended that practitioners thoroughly consider the motives underlying their spells and ensure they are consistent with this guiding concept. A spell meant to control or manipulate someone else against their will would not be deemed ethical, while a spell meant to heal or protect would.

Permission and respect for free will are other ethical factors when performing spells. Practitioners must obtain explicit agreement before attempting to control or interfere with another person's decisions and behaviors. This comprises spells that affect someone else's feelings, ideas, or actions. Spells with good intentions, like love or reconciliation spells, may have unexpected outcomes if they violate the participants' right to free will. Practitioners must uphold the autonomy and encourage individuals to make their own decisions.

The non-interference concept also applies to spells used in divination. Although many spiritual traditions use divination to gain insight and guidance, practitioners should proceed cautiously and humbly. It is immoral to snoop about other people's personal affairs or future directions without their permission, as this may infringe on their right to privacy and autonomy. Practitioners should instead concentrate on getting direction for themselves and enabling others to make decisions based on their agency and intuition.

Another ethical principle that drives spell craft in various traditions is the law of threefold return. According to this theory, any energy that a person releases into the universe —positive or negative—will return to them threefold. Practitioners are urged to check that the energy they use in their spells aligns with their aims and moral principles. This idea is a potent reminder of how everything is interrelated and how important it is to live a morally and compassionately upright life in all spheres of endeavor.

Practitioners should consider the broader ethical ramifications of their spell work in addition to these guiding concepts. This entails being aware of cultural appropriation and showing respect for the customs and traditions of other people. It is crucial to approach magical activities with respect, humility, and an open mind to different points of view. In addition, practitioners should consider how their spells affect the environment and make an effort to use ethically and sustainably sourced materials to reduce any adverse environmental effects.

In addition, practitioners need to be aware that casting spells may have unforeseen results. Energy is a strong force that can show up in surprising or unanticipated ways. As a result, spellcasters ought to approach the craft with humility and responsibility, understanding the intricacy of the forces they are working with and their limits. Whether the results of their spells are good or bad, they should be ready to accept responsibility for them, learn from them with humility and grace, and go on.

To sum up, ethical issues are crucial to spell work because they help practitioners utilize their magical skills honorably and responsibly. Practitioners can ensure that their spell work is done ethically and with good intent by abiding by principles like damage minimization, respect for free will, and alignment with universal values. By practicing mindfulness, humility, and a dedication to continuous learning and development, practitioners can utilize magic's transformational potential to bring about beneficial changes in their personal and external environments.

# CHAPTER IX

# Meditation and Visualization

## Techniques for meditation

The ancient practice of meditation, which has its roots in many spiritual and religious traditions, has become quite popular in modern culture because of its many positive effects on mental, emotional, and physical health. The variety of meditation approaches reflects the practice's complex history and cultural background. This section examines a few of the most well-known methods, emphasizing their unique qualities and advantages for users.

With its origins in Buddhist traditions, mindfulness meditation is one of the most popular types of meditation. Concentrating attention on the current moment without passing judgment is the goal of mindfulness meditation. Usually, practitioners begin by focusing on their breathing and paying attention to the intake and exhalation without attempting to regulate or change it. The meditator gradually returns the focus to the breath while acknowledging any ideas or feelings that occur without becoming attached to them. This method lessens stress and enhances focus by fostering a heightened awareness of the current moment. Mindfulness meditation is a valuable technique for treating anxiety and depression because it gradually promotes emotional stability and inner serenity.

Transcendental meditation (TM), which Maharishi Mahesh Yogi first taught in the middle of the 20th century, is another well-liked method. In Transcendental Meditation (TM), a practitioner uses a particular mantra—a word or phrase—that they repeat silently for fifteen to twenty minutes twice daily. Using the mantra, one can go beyond conventional thought and into a profoundly relaxed level of awareness. In contrast to mindfulness meditation, which stresses being aware of the present moment, transcendental meditation (TM) aims to create a pure consciousness by going beyond cognition. Research indicates that Transcendental Meditation (TM) is an effective method for people who want to achieve profound relaxation and mental clarity since it can dramatically lower blood pressure and stress levels and improve general mental health.

Metta meditation, or loving-kindness meditation, is a practice that focuses on developing compassion and unconditional love for both one and other people. This technique, which has its roots in Theravada Buddhism, silently repeats affirmations such as "May I be happy, may I be healthy, may I be safe, may I live with ease." The practitioner focuses on themselves and then progressively expands these intentions to include family, friends, strangers, and even people they disagree with. Loving-kindness meditation can improve emotional resilience, lessen negative emotions, and increase a sense of interconnectedness and empathy by cultivating a sense of universal love and compassion.

Zen Buddhism's foundational practice is Zen meditation or Zazen. This method strongly emphasizes sitting meditation, in which practitioners adopt a particular posture (usually the lotus or half-lotus) and concentrate on their breathing or a chosen koan, a paradoxical question or statement. Zen meditation seeks enlightenment and insight via firsthand experience instead of cerebral comprehension. It is recommended that practitioners keep an open and aware posture, letting thoughts come and go without attachment. Zen meditation promotes calmness and inner tranquility by facilitating significant insights into the essence of life and a deeper comprehension of the mind.

Guided meditation is an additional type of meditation in which you follow the instructions of a teacher or storyteller to enter a contemplative state. This method can be used in groups or alone, and it frequently incorporates gradual muscle relaxation, body scans, and visualization exercises. Beginners benefit most from guided meditation since it gives structure and direction, facilitating relaxation and concentration. The instructions and visuals might differ, addressing objectives like healing, stress relief, or personal development. Because of its adaptability, guided meditation may be used by people with many needs and preferences and is beneficial and accessible.

Another age-old method rooted in Buddhist tradition is vipassana meditation, sometimes called insight meditation. "To see things as they are" is the meaning of Vipassana, which entails a close, critical examination of one's feelings, ideas, and physical experiences. Initially, practitioners concentrate on their breathing. Gradually, they broaden their consciousness to include thoughts, emotions, and bodily sensations, observing them objectively and detachedly. Through developing a deep understanding of the transient and linked nature of all occurrences, this practice seeks to free oneself from pain and become wiser. Frequent Vipassana practice helps improve inner freedom, emotional control, and self-awareness.

In summary, a wide range of profound and diverse meditation practices offer a different path to mental, emotional, and spiritual well-being. People can find a meditation technique that speaks to their needs and goals, whether it is the focused awareness of mindfulness meditation, the profound transcendence of TM, the loving-kindness meditation, the direct insight of Zen meditation, the structured guidance of guided meditation, or the penetrating clarity of Vipassana. These methods, which are becoming more and more well-known, provide helpful resources for resolving the difficulties of contemporary life with more serenity, fortitude, and comprehension.

## Guided visualizations

A potent and transformational tool, guided visualizations are employed in many contexts, such as sports training, therapy, meditation, and personal growth. Using this method, a person or guide guides a person or group through a sequence of mental, visual, and tactile sensations. Guided visualizations are a flexible technique with several advantages that can affect emotions, thoughts, and bodily states by getting the mind going and concentrating on particular images or scenarios.

Fundamentally, guided visualization uses the brain's innate capacity to form rich, detailed mental images. The first step in this procedure is for the practitioner to become calm. This is frequently accomplished by deep breathing or gradually relaxing their muscles. After the person is at ease, the guide asks them to visualize a specific image or experience while offering thorough explanations to arouse their senses. To make the visualization experience as genuine and immersive as possible, these descriptions may include tastes, smells, sights, and tactile experiences. The secret to guided visualization's potency is its capacity to reach the subconscious mind, which contains ingrained emotions and beliefs. This opens the door to significant changes in perception and behavior.

Relaxation and stress reduction are two of the primary uses for guided visualizations. Guided visualizations can significantly reduce stress and foster a sense of serenity by taking people through quiet and pleasant settings, such as wandering through a forest, lying on a beach, or floating on a cloud. These visions' immersive quality aids in diverting the mind from daily anxieties and concerns, enabling the body to unwind and heal. According to studies, practicing guided visualizations regularly can improve physical and mental health by lowering stress hormone levels, blood pressure, and muscular tension.

Guided visualizations are frequently utilized in therapeutic settings to enhance mental health, emotional healing, and stress reduction. Therapists commonly use this method to assist their patients in processing challenging feelings, memories, or experiences in a secure setting. Using a guide, an individual can revisit a traumatic event and reframe and integrate the experience to facilitate healing and resolution. This is an example of guided visualization. By imagining good outcomes and reinforcing empowering ideas, this strategy can establish healthier coping skills, increase self-compassion, and raise self-esteem.

Guided visualizations are a standard tool performers and athletes use to improve their abilities and increase performance. Visualization techniques entail envisioning oneself executing a specific skill or reaching a desired goal. They are also known as mental rehearsal or imagery training. Muscle memory, coordination, and confidence are all enhanced by this mental practice, which stimulates the same brain pathways used in physical practice. For instance, a basketball player might see themselves consistently making the perfect shot, or a musician might see themselves playing a problematic piece flawlessly. Studies have indicated that athletes who integrate guided visualizations into their training regimens frequently report increased motivation, focus, and performance.

Additionally essential to goal achievement and personal growth are guided visions. People can increase their motivation and focus by seeing a clear future state, making it more straightforward to take concrete action toward their objectives. This method usually includes visualizing the specifics of accomplishing a goal, such as beginning a new job, finishing a project, or hitting a significant personal achievement. These visualizations can increase the likelihood of success by matching the subconscious mind with conscious aims through clarity and emotional engagement. Additionally, by identifying possible roadblocks and solutions, this method enables more efficient planning and problem-solving.

Guided visualizations are employed in spirituality and self-discovery to help people establish more robust bonds with the cosmos and their inner selves. These mental images could take the form of travels to visit a higher self, spirit guides, or symbolic landscapes that stand in for different facets of the mind. Such encounters can advance one's spiritual development and comprehension by offering perceptions, motivation, and a feeling of direction. These guided tours provide a means of developing a stronger sense of inner peace and fulfillment, connecting with others, and accessing inner wisdom for many people.

Moreover, guided visualizations can be an effective tool for ingenuity and originality. This method can dismantle mental obstacles and foster creative thought by pushing the mind to consider novel options. Guided visualizations are a standard tool authors, artists, and problem solvers use to unlock their creative potential and produce fresh viewpoints and ideas that might not come from traditional thought processes. Innovative ideas, improvements in artistic expression, and an increased ability to think creatively can all result from this creative research.

To sum up, guided visualizations are a flexible and valuable technique that may be used for various purposes, including stress relief, therapeutic healing, improving performance, personal growth, spiritual development, and creativity. Guided visualizations are powerful tools that can affect feelings, thoughts, and bodily states by using the imagination and concentrating on specific mental images. Those who practice them can reap significant benefits from them. As this method becomes more and more well-known, it offers a valuable tool for overcoming the challenges of contemporary life, promoting well-being, and realizing one's potential.

## Enhancing spiritual connection through mindfulness

In recent years, there has been a lot of interest in improving spiritual connection through mindfulness, which combines traditional spiritual practices with contemporary psychology knowledge. A significant route to increasing one's spiritual awareness and connection is mindfulness, which is the practice of being present and involved in the here and now. This section looks at mindfulness's concepts, practices, and potential transformational impacts on one's spiritual life to better understand how it can improve spiritual experiences.

The fundamental goal of mindfulness is to develop an honest, nonjudgmental awareness of the current moment. This means being aware of ideas, feelings, and experiences as they come to you without being caught up in them. By doing this, people can gain a better sense of clarity and understanding about their inner life and the outside world. In the context of spirituality, mindfulness aids people in tuning into a more profound awareness of their existence, which is frequently characterized as a relationship with the divine, the cosmos, or a higher self. Because of this increased consciousness, practitioners can discern spiritual significance in even the most routine actions by cultivating a feeling of holiness in ordinary situations.

A deep sense of present mindfulness is one of the main ways mindfulness improves spiritual connection. The value of being present is emphasized by spiritual traditions worldwide, whether through ritual, meditation, or prayer. This presence is directly fostered by mindfulness, which enables people to inhabit the present moment completely. By learning to examine thoughts and emotions without being attached, mindfulness practice makes room for a deeper relationship with life's spiritual side. One of the main ideas of many spiritual traditions, which frequently highlight the interconnectedness of all beings and the universe, is that people can experience a sense of unity with the cosmos through this presence.

Additionally, mindfulness strengthens spiritual ties by encouraging self-acceptance and self-awareness. Without passing judgment, people can observe their thoughts and feelings and gain an understanding of their genuine selves, including their desires, anxieties, strengths, and shortcomings. Being self-aware is essential to many spiritual approaches that stress understanding oneself and one's place in the cosmos through self-knowledge. Moreover, mindfulness cultivates a loving and compassionate relationship with oneself by promoting self-acceptance and self-compassion. A fundamental component of many spiritual traditions, this inner compassion frequently spills over into the outside world, strengthening one's ability to empathize and show empathy for others.

The capacity of mindfulness to induce inner calm and quiet the mind is another important feature of this practice. The fast-paced, constantly evolving modern world might make connecting with life's most profound spiritual aspects difficult. Meditation and mindful breathing are two techniques that can help quiet the mind and lessen mental chatter to foster inner calm and tranquility. Many claim to have had great spiritual revelations, a sensation of being connected to the divine, or moments of transcendence during this inner silence. People can connect with their spiritual intuition and listen to their inner wisdom in this peaceful environment.

By promoting an accepting and nonjudgmental outlook on life, mindfulness also aids in spiritual development. Spiritual traditions frequently stress the value of developing traits like humility, thankfulness, and open-mindedness. People who practice mindfulness learn to view their experiences with openness and inquiry instead of criticism and judgment. Their capacity for open-heartedness enables them to recognize the sacred in everything, deepening their understanding of life's wonder and beauty. Through an open-hearted acceptance of life's circumstances, people can enhance their spiritual practice and establish a closer connection with the divine presence in their lives.

Being aware can also improve people's relationships and strengthen their spiritual bonds with one another. People can develop more genuine and meaningful relationships by paying close attention to what others say and giving their full attention. Being present and paying attention fosters the development of compassion, understanding, and trust—all necessary for spiritual relationships. Numerous spiritual traditions hold that a person's connections reflect their spiritual condition. Mindfulness fosters these characteristics, enabling people to connect with others on a more profound, spiritual level.

Furthermore, integrating mindfulness with other spiritual practices can enhance and intensify their effects. Mindfulness improves these activities by adding a heightened awareness and presence to prayer, meditation, and ritual. For instance, practicing mindfulness during prayer can assist people in focusing more intently on their relationship with the divine and feeling a more profound sense of unity. Mindfulness makes deeper levels of reflection and understanding possible during meditation, which supports the maintenance of a clear and focused mind.

In conclusion, practicing mindfulness to improve spiritual connection is a powerful tool for anyone looking to go deeper spiritually. Through the cultivation of present, self-awareness, inner calm, open-heartedness, and meaningful relationships, mindfulness establishes a more profound connection with the spiritual realm and the divine. With its growing acceptance and appeal, mindfulness is a valuable tool for people who want to manage the challenges of contemporary life with more spiritual awareness, fulfillment, and serenity. By practicing mindfulness, one can discover the sacred in every moment, which enhances their spiritual development and helps them connect with the essence of life on a deeper level.

# CHAPTER X

# Divination Methods

## Tarot reading

Tarot reading is a centuries-old tradition that offers insights into a person's life and possible future by fusing aspects of spirituality, psychology, and mysticism. When invented in Europe in the middle of the 15th century, tarot cards were first employed for games, but they later evolved into instruments for self-analysis and divination. Tarot reading is becoming popular among those looking for direction, self-improvement, and a better understanding of who they are and where they're at in life.

Usually, a Tarot deck has 78 cards, separated into the Major Arcana and the Minor Arcana. There are 22 cards in the Major Arcana, and they all show important archetypal characters and symbolic settings. These cards stand for significant spiritual insights and transformative experiences. The Fool, The Magician, The High Priestess, and The World are examples. The 56 cards that make up the Minor Arcana are arranged into four suits: Wands, Cups, Swords, and Pentacles. Each suit is further divided into numbered cards and court cards (Page, Knight, Queen, and King), and each suit represents many facets of life, including creativity, emotions, intelligence, and material issues. Combined, these cards form a sophisticated system readers may decipher to uncover advice and insights.

A regular Tarot reading starts with the querent (the person requesting the reading) posing a question or focusing on a particular subject. The Tarot reader then chooses several cards to arrange in a specific layout, known as a spread, after shuffling the deck, frequently absorbing the energy of the questioner. The interaction between the meanings of each place in the spread and the individual cards creates a story. The Celtic Cross spread is a popular card arrangement with ten cards placed in a cross and staff pattern. It thoroughly analyzes the querent's circumstances, including previous influences, present difficulties, and possible results.

It takes a combination of intuitive understanding and familiarity with the customary interpretations of each card to interpret the cards. In addition to using their intuitive skills to identify deeper meanings and connections, tarot readers rely on their comprehension of the symbols, imagery, and themes included in the cards. This method calls for attention to the energy and situation of the querent and knowledge of the Tarot. Tarot reading is sometimes compared to storytelling by readers since the cards offer querent perspectives, clarity, and possible future directions by revealing various chapters and characters in their life stories.

A significant feature of Tarot reading is its capacity to encourage introspection and individual development. Through symbols and situations that speak to the querent's subconscious, Tarot can reveal sentiments, desires, and secret ideas. People who engage in this reflective process may become more self-aware and understanding, enabling them to make better judgments and live more confidently and clearly. Pulling the Tower card can suggest a time of turmoil that finally results in tremendous change and development while pulling The Lovers card might encourage the querent to consider their relationships and ideals.

Reading Tarot is highly prized for its ability to offer consolation and direction in uncertain or transitional times. The cards can provide comfort, draw attention to positive traits, and offer helpful solutions for problems.

Reading the Tarot cards helps them feel more connected to greater wisdom or intuitive knowledge, and it is a kind of spiritual support. Those who view Tarot reading as a means of accessing the collective unconscious or receiving messages from spiritual guidance sometimes highlight this spiritual aspect of the technique.

Despite its roots in mysticism, tarot reading has gained popularity among modern practitioners who take a psychological approach. Renowned psychologist Carl Jung saw the Tarot's potential for examining the human psyche and saw the archetypal images as reflections of universal patterns and inner processes. Incorporating Jungian notions into their interpretations, modern Tarot readers use the cards to facilitate personal transformation, comprehend psychological dynamics, and explore the inner self.

Critics of Tarot reading frequently dismiss it as simple superstition or pseudoscience, claiming that the interpretations are too nebulous or personal to have any real significance. Supporters respond, however, that the actual value of Tarot is not in its exact future predictiveness but in its power to provoke thought, awareness, and deliberate action. Whether considered a mystical ritual or a therapeutic aid, Tarot reading provides an exclusive and beneficial way to delve into the intricacies of life and acquire a better knowledge of oneself and one's journey.

To summarize, tarot reading is a complex art that uses intuition, symbolism, and archetypal imagery to offer direction and understanding. Readers can reveal previously unknown facets of the querent's life, encourage introspection, and provide comfort in uncertain times by using a Tarot deck. Tarot readings continue to enthrall and inspire people, whether viewed from a spiritual or psychological angle. They enable them to travel through life with more awareness and purpose. Tarot is still a potent and enduring practice in the modern world as a tool for self-discovery and progress.


## Scrying

Gazing into a reflecting surface or medium to obtain insight, predict the future, or unearth hidden knowledge is an old practice known as "scrying." Throughout ancient times, people have employed this divination technique to seek direction from what they believe to be spiritual or subconscious sources. Several objects can be used for scrying, such as fire, water, mirrors, crystal balls, and even smoke patterns. The fundamental component of scrying is the capacity to enter a meditative state, which permits the mind to unwind and open itself to visions, symbols, or messages that surface from the subconscious or the spirit realm.

Since scrying exists in many historical times and cultures, its beginnings take time to determine. Ancient societies like the Greeks, Romans, and Egyptians used scrying. Reflective surfaces or water were frequently used. Scrying became widespread in medieval Europe among mystics and alchemists who utilized mirrors and crystal balls to find answers to their practical and spiritual queries. Despite its mystical associations, scrying has frequently been seen with respect and skepticism, representing the human urge to investigate the unknown while being wary of its secrets.

The choice of medium always starts a scrying session. One of the earliest techniques is water scrying, which is staring into a bowl of water occasionally mixed with oil or ink to produce reflecting patterns. Mirror scrying uses a "black mirror," a darkened mirror, or a polished piece of obsidian. The most famous type of scrying is crystal ball scrying, which entails staring into a transparent or slightly opaque crystal sphere. While smoke scrying involves examining the forms and motions created by incense smoke, fire scrying requires gazing into a fire or candle's flames. Because each medium has unique qualities and customs, practitioners can select one that best suits their goals and inclinations.

Scrying calls for a clear, concentrated mind. A suitable atmosphere that is calm and devoid of distractions is usually the first thing practitioners do. Creating a religious atmosphere could entail burning incense, playing delicate music, or dim lighting. After that, the scryer enters a contemplative state, usually through deep breathing and relaxation exercises. The scryer fixes their sight on the selected medium, allowing their consciousness to drift and their vision to soften once their mind is calm and open. The intention is to transcend the medium's surface and enter a deeper consciousness where messages, symbols, or visions may manifest.

The medium may start taking on patterns or images as the scrying session continues. These visions are frequently delicate and intricate to discern without a strong intuitive sense. The scryer must let the dreams come to them without interfering or influencing the experience; instead, they must stay open and nonjudgmental. Through a greater connection with the subconscious mind or the spiritual realm, this passive method allows the scryer to gain insights that may not be available through conventional vision.

Scrying vision interpretations are highly subjective and differ greatly based on the practitioner's objectives, background, and beliefs. While some scryers see distinct, prominent images, others pick up on abstract patterns or symbols that need more thought and examination. These visions' meanings are frequently subjective, influenced by the scryer's experiences and viewpoints. But some common symbols and archetypes appear in scrying; for example, fire symbolizes transformation and water represents emotions. The scryer must rely on their inner intelligence and intuition to interpret the messages and apply them to their questions or lives.

There are many reasons to weep, from self-reflection to asking for advice on particular problems. Some use it as a spiritual development and self-discovery tool, providing insights into their inner world and the larger universe. Others use scrying as a divination to obtain insight or understanding into what is ahead. In either scenario, the practice promotes a closer relationship with the intuitive self and a heightened consciousness of the subtle dynamics at work in one's life. This increased awareness has the potential to bring about significant changes that give people the confidence and insight to manage their paths better.

Scrying has drawn criticism and skepticism despite its mystical appeal, especially from rationalist and scientific viewpoints. Some who criticize scrying claim that the images result from the imagination or the brain's inclination to identify patterns in seemingly random information. These criticisms draw attention to the practice's subjectivity but do not always take away from its worth. The insights obtained through scrying have a profound and lasting effect on many practitioners, giving them a sense of purpose and connection beyond empirical validation.

In summary, scrying is a vast and diverse technique that connects the fields of spirituality, psychology, and mysticism. By looking into reflecting materials and meditating, practitioners aim to gain insight, reveal hidden truths, and establish deeper connections with the universe and themselves. Scrying provides a singular means of delving into the unknown and accepting life's mysteries, regardless of whether it is perceived as a mystical art form or a contemplative tool. Like any spiritual practice, its worth is found in individual discoveries and transformations, leading people to a deeper understanding of themselves.

## Other divinatory tools (Runes, Pendulum, etc.)

For millennia, humans have used supernatural methods to seek knowledge of the future or the unknown, a technique known as divination. Although scrying and tarot cards are two of the most popular divination aids, people employ many additional methods to obtain wisdom and direction. This section examines a few of these lesser-known instruments, such as pendulums, runes, the I Ching, and reading tea leaves, emphasizing their historical contexts, practical applications, and distinctive contributions to the field of divination.

Runes are a traditional divination tool with roots in Germanic and Norse cultures. By definition, the word "rune" denotes "secret" or "mystery." Each of the 24 symbols comprising a set of runes is usually etched onto a little piece of bone, stone, or wood. These characters, collectively called the Elder Futhark, each have a unique meaning and are thought to be the oldest form of the runic alphabet. When using runes for divination, a practitioner can cast multiple runes to understand a situation better or draw a single rune to answer a particular query. Understanding the symbolic meanings of each symbol and how they relate to one another is necessary for rune interpretation. This practice uses archetypal energies and old wisdom to bring insights into many areas of life, including relationships, personal struggles, and future occurrences.

Another popular divination equipment that is renowned for its adaptability and simplicity is the pendulum. A pendulum is a small weight, usually a crystal or metal object, suspended from a chain or string. With the pendulum in hand, the practitioner poses a question and lets it swing freely. The answers to the questions are deduced from the direction and motion of the pendulum, whether it swings in a circle, side to side, or back and forth. According to popular belief, the pendulum connects with spiritual or subconscious forces, providing information based on minute physical cues or energetic vibrations. It is frequently used to find things, ask yes-or-no inquiries, and identify energy imbalances in the body.

The "Book of Changes," known as the I Ching, has been a widely utilized divination tool in ancient China for over three millennia. The 64 hexagrams of this design are six lines that can be broken (yang) or unbroken (yin). When consulting the I Ching, a practitioner typically creates a hexagram with coins or yarrow stalks, which is then interpreted using the text's copious commentary. Every hexagram represents a particular circumstance or condition and offers direction for overcoming the obstacles and seizing the opportunities that lie ahead. The I Ching provides insightful philosophical analysis and helpful guidance, emphasizing the fluidity of life and the value of adjusting to change.

The divination practice of "tea leaf reading," or "tasseography," involves analyzing patterns in tea leaves that remain in a cup after the tea has been sipped. This custom dates back to ancient China, and in the 17th and 18th centuries, it became increasingly common in Europe. The querent sips a cup of loose-leaf tea, leaving a tiny bit of liquid at the bottom for a tea leaf reading. After giving the cup a quick twist, the leftover leaves are let to settle. Using their imagination and sense of intuition, the reader deciphers the meanings and messages in the shapes and patterns the leaves have formed. Every shape or symbol offers unique and creative advice since it is connected to various facets of life, such as love, health, or work.

Another old-fashioned divination method is astrology, which uses the positions and motions of celestial bodies to shed light on human affairs. Astrologers record the positions of the planets and their aspects to one another to generate birth charts based on the precise time, date, and location of an individual's birth. After that, these charts are examined to identify personality qualities, recurring themes in life, and probable future occurrences. Numerous systems and traditions are included in astrology, including Chinese, Vedic, and Western astrology, each with distinct techniques and interpretations. Astrology can provide more general forecasts regarding global events and social trends, even though it is frequently utilized for personal readings.

Studying the mystical meaning of numbers, or numerology, is another divination method for unearthing secrets and insights. Numerologists analyze a person's name and birthday to determine their life path, personality, and destiny by analyzing the numbers connected to those details. It is said that every number has a unique vibrational energy and symbolic meaning that affects various facets of life. By comprehending these numerical patterns, people can better grasp their advantages, disadvantages, and chances.

Reading a person's handwriting to learn about their personality and future is known as palmistry or chiromancy. This custom originates in antiquated societies, such as Greece, China, and India. Palmists examine the shape and size of the fingers, mounts, and other features in addition to the principal lines on the palm, such as the headline, lifeline, and heart line. Because every feature on the hand is linked to distinct characteristics and life events, a palmist can deliver a comprehensive and unique reading.

In conclusion, divination instruments like runes, pendulums, the I Ching, tea leaf reading, astrology, numerology, and palmistry have many different and rich ways to seek direction and insight. Every tool has a distinct history, method, and symbolic system that represents how people have attempted to connect with the divine, develop their intuition, and solve the riddles of life. These skills offer invaluable insights, enabling people to navigate their lives with greater clarity, confidence, and a sense of connectedness to the broader world, regardless of whether they are viewed as mystical arts or psychological practices. Divination is still a potent and reliable way to delve into the unknown and reveal the knowledge that lies within, even as it develops further.

# CHAPTER XI

# Working with Nature and Elements

## The significance of the four elements

For millennia, the idea of the four elements—Earth, water, air, and fire—has been a fundamental part of scientific, philosophical, and spiritual thinking. These components, which have their roots in ancient societies and have endured through many traditions, stand for essential ideas that are thought to make up the physical cosmos and impact human existence. The four elements have meaning beyond their actual characteristics; they represent many facets of life and the human experience and offer a framework for comprehending the natural world and our place in it.

Empedocles was the first to explain the four elements of ancient Greek philosophy systematically. He maintained that these fundamental components make up all matter. Later, Aristotle developed this theory by associating certain traits with each element: fire was connected with dryness and heat, water with wetness and coolness, earth with dryness and heat, and air with wetness and heat. These components were combined in Aristotle's idea to produce a dynamic system of transformation, which implied that these components may convert into one another through heating and cooling. This essential conception shaped Western thought for centuries and served as a foundation for early scientific investigation.

Apart from their tangible characteristics, the four elements hold profound symbolic implications in many spiritual and mystical traditions. For example, Earth is frequently linked to materialism, grounding, and stability. It stands for the physical form, the environment, and the basis of all existence. Earth is revered as the benevolent mother who gives life and support in many civilizations. This component fosters traits like endurance, patience, and practicality and reminds people to maintain a connection to the material world.

Conversely, water represents feelings, instincts, and the subconscious. Because of its fluidity and adaptability, water can take on several shapes, ranging from the smooth flow of a stream to the intense fury of a storm. Water is frequently associated with healing, purification, and the depths of the human mind. It helps people connect with their deepest emotions and explore their inner worlds by promoting emotional expression and introspection. Water is often employed in rites of purification and rebirth in spiritual practices, indicating its transformational properties.

The domain of ideas, communication, and intellectual endeavors is symbolized by air. It is linked to the life-giving breath and the unseen forces that bind all living things together. Air promotes communication, creativity, and clarity. The motivating and enlightening component fosters mental flexibility and the capacity for multiple viewpoints. In many cultures, air is associated with the spirit and the higher mind, implying a relationship between spiritual enlightenment and cerebral pursuits.

The most energetic element, fire, represents vigor, passion, and change. It is a force that can both create and destroy, able to both light up and devour. Fire is a metaphor for the passion and drive that spur people on to success and ignite their creative and motivational sparks. It is linked to determination, bravery, and the ability to take action. Fire frequently represents purification and the presence of heavenly energy in spiritual circumstances. Candle lighting and bonfire rituals are two examples of fire-related rituals that call forth spiritual force and promote personal transformation.

How the four elements interact illustrates the necessity for harmony and balance in the natural world and human existence. A dynamic system is created when all the elements work together to balance and complement one another, preventing any one factor from dominating. This harmony may be seen in many different disciplines, including traditional Chinese medicine, which uses the five elements—Earth, water, fire, air, and wood—to explain health and illness. The four elements are also utilized in astrology to categorize zodiac signs and comprehend personality features, highlighting the necessity of a harmonious fusion of various energies.

For human development and self-awareness, the four elements remain potent symbols in modern spiritual and psychological activities. They provide a comprehensive framework for investigating various facets of the self and reaching equilibrium. For example, if someone is feeling unsteady, they can be urged to cultivate the anchoring qualities of Earth, or if they are looking for change, they might be encouraged to embrace the transforming force of fire. Working with the elements helps people develop a sense of wholeness and harmony by assisting them to connect with the world and themselves on a deeper level.

The four components also offer a way to reconnect with the natural world and surroundings. The elemental framework serves as a reminder of people's inherent connection to the Earth, water, air, and fire at a time when technological improvements frequently cause people to feel disconnected from the natural world. This knowledge can promote sustainable practices and a more profound respect for the planet's resources by fostering a higher sense of stewardship and responsibility towards the environment.

The meaning of the four elements—Earth, water, air, and fire—goes far beyond how they appear on the surface. They provide insights into the essence of life and the interdependence of all things, serving as fundamental principles that influence both the natural world and the human experience. The elements offer a rich framework for spiritual development, environmental awareness, and human progress because of their symbolic connotations and dynamic interplay. As timeless archetypes, they never stop encouraging and directing people toward harmony, balance, and a more profound comprehension of the cosmos.

## Elemental correspondences and rituals

Many magical, religious, and spiritual traditions have long included elemental correspondences and rituals. These correspondences provide the four classical elements—earth, water, air, and fire—with specific metaphorical qualities and meanings. By comprehending and applying these relationships, practitioners can design rituals that utilize the distinct energies of each component to accomplish spiritual, emotional, and physical objectives. The elements offer a rich framework for individual transformation and reconnection with the natural forces, acting as potent archetypes that span the gap between the material and spiritual realms.

Earth is connected to materialism, solidity, and grounding. The body, the natural world, and everything tangibly represented are all included in the physical domain. Earth's correspondences include soil, vegetation, stones and crystals, and green color. In ceremonies, Earth energy is called upon to provide security, plenty, and safety. Planting seeds to represent growth and fresh starts or erecting a sacred area with stones and crystals to ground and shield the energy within our everyday Earth rituals. These rites are frequently carried out outside or in other natural settings to strengthen the bond with the earth element.

Water is a symbol of feelings, instincts, and the subconscious. It can take on several shapes, ranging from the soft trickle of a stream to the forceful cascade of a waterfall due to its fluidity and adaptability. Water is represented by the color blue, sea salt, shells, and many types of water, including rivers, lakes, and seas. Water rituals frequently incorporate emotional release, healing, and purification. Two examples of cleansing rituals are bathing in a natural body of water or making a sacred bath with salts and herbs to remove negative energy. Meditation near bodies of water can also facilitate connecting with one's emotions and developing intuition. Water rituals are very effective for people trying to find emotional equilibrium and clarity.

The domain of ideas, communication, and intellectual endeavors is symbolized by air. It is linked to the life-giving breath and the unseen forces that bind all living things together. The color yellow, feathers, incense, and the wind are all associated with air. Air rituals frequently center on communication, inspiration, and mental clarity. Practitioners can improve mental focus and cleanse an area using essential oils or incense. Affirmations that are written or spoken into the wind can represent the spread of ideas and goals. Air rituals are great for cerebral growth, creativity stimulation, and communication ability improvement.

Fire is a sign representing vigor, passion, and change. It can create, destroy, consume, purify, and provide warmth and light. The color red, candles, bonfires, and the sun are all associated with fire. Rituals using fire are frequently conducted to evoke bravery, passion, and transformation. Daily fire rituals include lighting candles while concentrating on a particular objective and gathering around a bonfire to burn anxieties or old habits holding you back. Fire rituals work very well for people who want to embrace change, ignite motivation, or purify and cleanse their lives.

Several cultures combine all four elements into extensive ceremonies in addition to elemental rituals to attain harmony and balance. For instance, the elements are frequently invoked in forming a holy circle in Wiccan and Pagan traditions. Each of the four cardinal points—north for earth, east for air, south for fire, and west for water—may represent the elements placed there by practitioners. As a result, a safe, balanced area is created where the energies of all the elements can be combined and used.

Numerous healing techniques also use elemental correspondences. For example, crystal healing involves choosing stones that match particular components and applying them to the body to balance energy. Essential oils linked to various elements are used in aromatherapy to affect mental and physical conditions. These techniques demonstrate the adaptability and strength of elemental energies in fostering spiritual development and well-being.

The components also provide a framework for comprehending the rhythms and cycles of nature. Many civilizations observe seasonal festivals as a way of paying tribute to the shifting elemental energies of the year. For instance, the summer solstice is connected to fire, signifying the height of vigor and energy. In contrast, the spring equinox is frequently connected to the earth element, symbolizing rebirth and fresh development. These festivities highlight the interdependence of humanity and the natural world and the significance of living in balance with the planet's cycles.

The application of elemental correspondences and rituals is a universal practice seen in many spiritual pathways and cultures, not limited to any one school. Interacting with the elements enables people to access age-old knowledge and establish a connection with the fundamental forces that form the universe, whether via the thoughtful arrangement of stones, the lighting of a candle, or meditation by a river. This relationship reminds us of our essential role in the larger scheme of things and helps us feel greater understanding and belonging.

To sum up, elemental correspondences and rituals offer a potent way to connect with nature and use its forces for spiritual and psychological development. Earth, water, air, and fire are the elements. Each has unique qualities and meanings, providing different means to achieve stability, emotional equilibrium, mental clarity, and transforming energy. People can develop a more profound sense of self-awareness, attain a harmonious balance, and harmonize with the universe's natural cycles by implementing these components into their rituals and practices. This age-old knowledge is still relevant today because it provides a timeless framework for understanding and accepting the interconnection of all life.

## Connecting with nature spirits

An age-old custom shared by many nations and traditions connects with nature spirits, reflecting humanity's persistent yearning to communicate with the natural world's invisible forces. The guardians and embody of the natural world's elements and landscapes are said to be nature spirits, sometimes known as elementals, faeries, or devas. These creatures, each with distinct energy and personality, are believed to exist in forests, rivers, mountains, and other natural places. To establish communication with nature spirits, one must combine spiritual awareness, reverence for the natural world, and specific rituals or meditation practices.

Establishing a closer bond with the planet and its ecosystems is one of the main motivations behind people's search for connections with nature spirits. A stronger sense of care and obligation for the preservation of the environment might result from this connection, which can heighten one's enjoyment. Indigenous civilizations have long acknowledged the existence of nature spirits and included them in their spiritual practices. Examples of these cultures are Native American and Aboriginal traditions. These cultures frequently see natural spirits as essential members of their societies who offer wisdom, protection, and guidance. People pay respect to these spirits through ceremonies and offerings, preserving their healthy relationship with the natural world.

Practitioners frequently start by selecting a natural location with a deep sense of serenity and connection to establish a connection with nature spirits. This can be a serene riverbank, a remote woodland, or a magnificent peak. Once in this environment, it's critical to approach with reverence and sincerity. Many people think people who genuinely love and appreciate the environment will have a higher chance of seeing nature spirits. One can indicate their wish to respect and establish a connection with the spirits of a location by doing modest gestures like tidying up trash, chatting politely with trees, or bringing a small gift of food or flowers.

Mindfulness and meditation are essential practices for connecting with nature spirits. Practitioners frequently sit silently in their preferred natural environment, paying attention to their breathing and letting their thoughts drift. This condition of heightened awareness and inner calm might facilitate perceiving the presence of nature, spirits, and subtle energies. Some claim that a light wind, a slight whisper, or a change in the atmosphere can sense the presence of nature spirits. It can also be beneficial to use visualization techniques, such as seeing a protective circle of light around oneself or having a heart-to-heart conversation with a nearby tree's spirit.

The use of rituals and ceremonies is essential when trying to communicate with natural spirits. These might be anything from straightforward everyday routines to intricate seasonal festivities. Making a nature altar, a tiny sacred area decorated with organic items like stones, leaves, feathers, and flowers, is one widespread practice. This shrine helps to synchronize one's energy with the natural world by acting as a focal point for offerings and meditation. Celebrating the solstices and equinoxes, which are periods of increased natural energy, is one example of a seasonal ritual. To respect the land's spirits and ask for their blessings, practitioners may burn candles, chant, or dance during these ceremonies.

It's thought that some herbs and plants have unique qualities that make it easier to communicate with nature spirits. For example, in smudging ceremonies, sage and cedar are frequently used to cleanse the area and draw positive energies. Mugwort is sometimes burned as incense or brewed into tea before attempting to contact nature spirits because of its reputation for enhancing psychic awareness. You can also utilize essential oils and flower essences to attune to the unique vibrations of various nature spirits. Respectfully and thoughtfully using these organic instruments can create a sacred space that fosters spiritual intimacy.

Each person's experience of communicating with nature spirits is unique. Some people may experience intense visual encounters in which they perceive the spirits as personifications of the elements or as ethereal creatures of light. Others may get messages through dreams and coincidences or have an intuitive sense of presence. The secret is to have faith in one's senses and keep an open mind about the nuanced ways nature's spirits speak to us. Deepening sensitivity and consistent practice over time can result in deeper and more meaningful connections.

The advantages of communicating with nature spirits go beyond fostering one's spiritual development. Many discover these relationships give them a stronger feeling of contentment, joy, and belonging. They frequently have a revitalized sense of purpose and drive to preserve nature. People can become more in tune with the cycles and rhythms of the planet and live more harmoniously and in balance by developing a relationship with the spirits of nature. This link can also improve the ability to access inner wisdom and guidance since nature spirits are frequently viewed as allies on the path of spiritual and personal development.

In summary, communicating with nature spirits is a very fulfilling activity that helps to bridge the gap between the material and spiritual worlds. It entails employing natural tools to heighten one's spiritual sensitivity, practicing attentive meditation and rituals, and developing a sense of appreciation for the natural environment. The intention is to become receptive to the knowledge and presence of these unseen protectors of nature, whether through elaborate ceremonies or moments of introspection. Doing this can create a deep sense of healing, harmony, and connection with the planet and its living forms. This age-old practice is still relevant today, providing insightful guidance and motivation to individuals who want to strengthen their bond with the natural world.

# CHAPTER XII

# Healing and Herbal Magic

## Basics of herbalism

Using plants for medical purposes or herbalism has been a fundamental component of human healthcare for thousands of years. It includes various customs and methods, from modern Western herbalism to antiquated systems like Traditional Chinese Medicine (TCM) and Ayurveda. Herbalism continues to be a well-liked and successful strategy for health and wellness despite advancements in contemporary medicine. The fundamentals of herbalism include knowing the characteristics and applications of different herbs, how to prepare and apply herbal treatments, and the holistic health care tenets that support this field of medicine.

Fundamentally, herbalism rests on the understanding that many chemical substances found in plants can be therapeutically beneficial to human health. These substances, which include tannins, alkaloids, flavonoids, and essential oils, have various therapeutic and calming effects on the body. To better understand these substances and their effects, herbalists consult modern scientific research and traditional wisdom. For example, although willow bark has long been used as a pain reliever, modern science discovered salicin, a chemical found in willow bark, to be the predecessor to aspirin.

The categorization of herbs based on how they affect the body is one of the core ideas of herbalism. Adaptogens—which aid in the body's ability to handle stress—anti-inflammatories—which lessen inflammation—antimicrobials—which fend off infections—and nervines—which assist the neurological system—are typical categories. Herbalists can customize their remedies to meet the unique needs of their patients by having a thorough understanding of these categories and how certain herbs fit into them. For instance, adaptogenic herbs such as Rhodiola or ashwagandha may help someone under a lot of stress, and echinacea or elderberry may help someone with a cold by strengthening their immune system.

There are numerous varieties of herbal remedies, each suitable for a particular purpose and taste. Two popular methods for preparing plants are decoctions and infusions. Like brewing tea, an infusion steers plants in hot water and is usually used for sensitive plant components like leaves and blossoms. Conversely, decoctions need to be boiled with the therapeutic qualities of more complex plant parts like bark and roots, decoctiger, and the more durable alternative is tinctures, concentrated extracts created by soaking herbs in vinegar or alcohol. Topical applications include salves and ointments, which are made by blending oils and spices that have been infused with beeswax. Every preparation technique has benefits and is selected according to the specific plant and intended medicinal outcome.

Herbalism's holistic approach is one of its distinguishing characteristics. Herbalists try to promote the body's natural healing processes and comprehend the underlying causes of illness rather than just treating the symptoms. This method looks at the whole person—body, mind, and spirit—and how lifestyle, nutrition, and mental health affect overall health and illness. Herbalists generally spend a great deal of time getting to know their patients, gathering comprehensive medical histories, and creating individualized therapy regimens that target the underlying causes of their health problems. Results from this patient-centered approach may be more long-lasting and productive.

In herbalism, safety and effectiveness are of utmost importance. While most individuals find most herbs to be safe and gentle, some may have adverse effects or interact negatively with pharmaceuticals. Herbalists need to understand the pharmacology of plants and be cautious of any possible side effects. This entails being aware of appropriate dosages, contraindications, and the unique requirements of various demographics, including the elderly, children, and pregnant women. Maintaining safe and efficient practices requires ongoing education and remaining current with research findings.

The sustainability of natural resources and the environment are closely related to herbalism. Ethical sourcing and sustainable harvesting methods are essential to ensure that medicinal plant usage does not destroy ecosystems or deplete wild populations. To increase biodiversity and lessen the strain on wild populations, many herbalists support growing medicinal plants in farms and gardens. The herbalist community holds environmental stewardship in high regard, as it reflects an immense dedication to the earth's health and the well-being of individual patients.

Herbalism includes both self-care and education as essential elements. Many people learn about common herbs and how to use them for common conditions, turning to herbalism to take control of their health. Herbal education comes in various formats, from self-study and community seminars to official training programs and apprenticeships. By arming people with information about medicinal herbs, herbalism encourages a sense of agency and self-reliance in healthcare.

To sum up, the foundations of herbalism comprise an intricate and rich history that incorporates an understanding of plant chemistry, techniques of preparation, holistic health concepts, and environmental sustainability. Herbalism emphasizes the body's innate ability to heal and the significance of treating the underlying causes of sickness, providing a natural and approachable approach to healthcare. Herbalism is an essential and relevant practice in the modern world, whether via the thorough study of plant properties, the manufacture of herbal treatments, or the cultivation of a deeper relationship with nature. The ancient wisdom of herbalism offers a timeless and flexible foundation for attaining wholeness and harmony as interest in natural and holistic health develops.

## Healing spells and practices

Spells and rituals for healing have long been a component of human society, including many different traditions and worldviews. These practices encourage mental, emotional, and spiritual well-being through ritual, intention, and spiritual energy. Healing spells and practices are found worldwide in religious and spiritual practices, although they are frequently connected to magical or occult traditions. Fundamentally, they represent the idea that spiritual energies can promote healing on all levels and that the mind, body, and spirit are interrelated.

Manipulating energy is a fundamental tenet of healing spells and practices. Practitioners hold that a subtle energy field, sometimes known as chi, prana, or life force, exists within all living things. Healing spells and practices are intended to bring harmony and balance back to the body's energy system, as illness and sickness are perceived as disturbances or obstructions in this energy flow. This energy is channeled and directed using visualization, chanting, and ritual to support health and vitality.

Symbols, herbs, crystals, and other tools are used in many healing spells and practices to focus and magnify purpose. Using runes, sigils, or sacred geometry, for instance, in spellwork can assist in encoding particular intentions and establishing a structure to manifest healing energy. Because of their therapeutic powers and energy aspects, herbs and plants are frequently employed in healing rituals. Gemstones and crystals are well-liked instruments for healing work since it is thought that their particular vibrational frequencies might affect the body's energy field.

Visualization is a potent tool in healing rituals and spells that helps focus energy and activate the body's natural healing processes. Practitioners can picture a particular result, like cells in the body healing and renewing themselves, or they can picture light or energy coursing through the body, dispelling obstacles and bringing about equilibrium. Deeply relaxing and healing can also be achieved through guided imagery and meditation. Practitioners can activate the body's innate ability to heal by using their thoughts.

Another crucial component of healing rituals and practices is sound and vibration. Harmonious vibrations are produced by chanting, toning, and singing bowls; these vibrations resonate with the body's energy centers, or chakras, fostering alignment and balance. The foundation of sound healing is that various frequencies can significantly impact the body and mind, lowering stress levels, encouraging healing, and eliciting states of relaxation. By attuning to the body's inherent rhythms through sound, practitioners can promote healing on a subtle yet profound level.

In many healing spells and practices, ceremony and ritual are essential components. Rituals create a holy environment where healing can occur by offering a framework for energy work and intention-setting. Candles, incense, and other symbolic objects are frequently used to focus intention and raise the energy level of the ritual. Practitioners can strengthen their connection to the healing process and seek spiritual guidance and help by carrying out rituals with reverence and attention.

Spells and rituals for healing are not just for the individual; they can also be applied to help heal the globe or the collective. Rituals and ceremonies in groups are frequently conducted to provide healing energy to particular people, communities, or even the Earth. These rituals produce healing and transformational effects through the communal power of intention. Practitioners can magnify the healing energy and effect positive change on a grander scale by uniting in solidarity and common purpose.

A crucial component of healing rituals and practices is ethical thought. When doing any healing work, practitioners must always respect the autonomy and free will of the people they are dealing with, getting their permission first. Additionally, it's critical to approach healing rituals and spells with humility, honoring the intricacies of the human body and the mysteries surrounding the healing process. Although spiritual healing can be a potent adjunct to traditional medical care, it should never replace qualified medical care. Instead, practitioners should always advise clients to obtain the proper medical care when necessary.

In summary, healing rituals and spells effectively advance peace, health, and well-being in all spheres of life. Practitioners can assist in healing on a physical, emotional, and spiritual level by combining ritual, intention, and spiritual energy. These methods acknowledge the connection of mind, body, and spirit through a holistic treatment approach that draws from traditional knowledge and contemporary insights. Healing spells and practices offer a significant road to healing and transformation for individuals and communities, whether through sound healing, visualization, or ceremonial ritual.

## Creating herbal remedies and potions

Making potions and herbal medicines is a long-standing custom that originated in ancient cultures and is still quite popular today. Herbal remedies provide a natural and comprehensive approach to health and wellness by utilizing plants' therapeutic qualities to treat various physical, mental, and spiritual illnesses. Herbal treatments come in many forms, each with specific uses and advantages, ranging from tinctures and teas to salves and syrups. The art and science of making herbal medicines and potions are examined in this section, covering everything from choosing and chopping plants to formulating robust and efficient concoctions.

Choosing the right plants for the intended purpose is the first step in making herbal treatments. Herbalists select herbs based on a wealth of botanical information and traditional wisdom to meet the individual needs of their patients or clientele. A person's constitution and symptoms are considered, along with the plant's medicinal virtues, energetic attributes, and contraindications. Certain herbs are appreciated for their capacity to boost the immune system or stimulate circulation, while others are known for their calming and soothing properties. Herbalists can design specialized formulas that treat the underlying causes of health disorders and enhance overall well-being by understanding the distinctive qualities of each herb.

Following their selection, the herbs are processed in several ways to extract their therapeutic properties. One of the most popular techniques is making herbal teas or infusions, which entail steeping plants in hot water to extract their health benefits. Due to their mild and calming properties, teas are frequently used to treat various ailments, from stress and anxiety to digestive problems. Making tinctures, which entails soaking plants in vinegar or alcohol to extract their active ingredients, is another well-liked technique. Tinctures are practical and adaptable for various herbal compositions since they are highly concentrated and long-lasting.

Herbal medicines come in various forms besides teas and tinctures, such as salves, oils, syrups, and capsules. Herbs are infused into a carrier oil, like olive or coconut oil, and then combined with beeswax to form salves and oils, which are therapeutic balms or ointments. These topical medicines are used for wound healing, muscle soreness, and skin disorders. Herbs make syrups a tasty and calming treatment for respiratory infections, sore throats, and coughs. The spices are simmered in water, and sweeteners like honey or maple syrup are added. Herbs are dried, ground into a fine powder, and placed within capsules for easy and accurate administration.

Herbal treatments' potency and effectiveness are contingent upon various aspects, such as the quality of the herbs, the preparation technique, and the dosage and frequency of administration. Purchasing herbs from reliable vendors who value organic farming, sustainability, and humane harvesting methods is crucial. Carefully planted and picked fresh or dried herbs will hold onto their medicinal properties and effectiveness, making the cures more potent. A therapeutic dosage of active ingredients is guaranteed in the finished product by employing appropriate preparation techniques, such as utilizing the correct ratio of herbs to water or alcohol and adhering to suggested extraction timeframes. To ensure safe and effective therapy, herbalists also consider individual parameters such as age, weight, and health state when calculating dosage and frequency of administration.

Herbal cures and potions not only have the ability to heal physically but also have subtle energy effects that support harmony and balance on a deeper level. Herbal medicine is recognized to benefit significantly from energetics, and many traditional therapeutic systems, like Ayurveda and Traditional Chinese Medicine, categorize herbs based on their energetic properties, which can include warming, cooling, drying, or moistening. These energetic attributes are thought to work in concert with the body's inherent energy field, or chi, to support health and vigor while reestablishing homeostasis. Practitioners can formulate herbal remedies that help holistic healing by considering both the treatments' physical and energy components.

Herbal medicine and potion creation are both an art and a science, needing intuition, ability, and understanding to create potent and effective formulas. Herbalists choose, prepare, and administer herbs to support health and well-being by drawing on a rich tapestry of botanical expertise, traditional knowledge, and contemporary research. Herbal medicines, whether in teas and tinctures, salves and syrups, capsules and oils, or other forms, provide a safe, all-natural method of healing that respects the connection between the mind, body, and spirit. The appreciation of the vast healing potential of plants and the craft of making herbal medicines and potions is growing along with interest in herbal therapy.

# CHAPTER XIII

# Living a Wiccan Lifestyle

**Incorporating Wiccan principles into daily routines**

A person's life can be significantly enhanced by incorporating Wiccan concepts into everyday activities. This can lead to a stronger sense of spirituality, self-awareness, and connection with nature. Fundamentally, Wicca is a contemporary pagan religion that emphasizes magickal activity, devotion to the divine in all its forms, and respect for the Earth and her cycles. While Wiccan ceremonies and rituals are frequently held on particular moon phases or Sabbaths, incorporating Wiccan ideas into everyday life can provide a constant source of empowerment and direction. Believing in the interconnection of all living things and the significance of living in harmony with nature are two core tenets of Wicca. You can incorporate this idea into your daily practice by practicing thankfulness and attention toward the natural world. We may effectively be reminded of our connection to the Earth and the divine by setting aside some time each day to appreciate the wonders of nature, such as the aroma of blooming flowers, the rustle of leaves in the wind, or the majesty of the sunrise.

One central tenet of Wicca is "As above, so below; as within, so without." This principle highlights that our microcosms mirror the universe's macrocosms and vice versa. To integrate this idea into our everyday lives, we must develop self-awareness and ensure our behaviors are consistent with our spiritual values. Deepening this connection through self-reflection, journaling, or meditation can help us identify life patterns and make conscious decisions consistent with our beliefs. Incorporating rituals like candle lighting, incense burning, or setting up altars for particular aims can also be concrete reminders of our spiritual objectives.

Wicca also highlights the significance of respecting the divine in its manifestations, including the god, the goddess, and other deities from many cultural traditions. Including worshiping gods in everyday activities can be prayers, sacrifices, or just spending time in meditation or imagination to communicate with the divine. Through developing a close relationship with a deity, practitioners can get support, direction, and ideas from outside the physical world.

Wicca also promotes magic usage to bring about beneficial changes in one's life and the wider world. Even though spells and magical rituals are frequently connected to particular objectives or intents, magic can also be incorporated into everyday activities by doing straightforward energy work, affirmations, and visualization exercises. Using the intention to produce a significant change in our lives can be achieved by setting intentions every morning, picturing desired results, and infusing ordinary activities with magical intent.

Incorporating Wiccan ideas into daily life is a road to personal strength and progress and a method to live according to one's spiritual beliefs. Wiccans can face life's obstacles with grace and grit by practicing mindfulness, self-awareness, and a profound respect for nature. People can materialize their greatest wishes and reach their potential by practicing magick, meditation, and daily rituals. Applying Wiccan teachings to everyday life is a path of self-awareness and metamorphosis that results in increased spiritual and personal fulfillment, balance, and harmony.

## Eco-friendly and sustainable living

Living a sustainable and environmentally friendly lifestyle is becoming increasingly important today, as dangers to the globe and future generations arise from climate change and environmental degradation. The term "sustainable living" refers to various actions and way of life decisions that lessen our environmental impact and foster harmony with the natural world. Fundamentally, sustainable living entails making deliberate choices that put social justice, economic viability, and ecological preservation first. A fundamental principle of environmentally conscious living is cutting back on waste and consumption. This can entail leading simple lives, buying things with little to no packaging, and giving reusable items priority over disposable ones. People can significantly lessen their environmental effects and help conserve natural resources by cutting back on their consumption and opting for products made of sustainable materials.

Reducing energy use and utilizing renewable energy sources is another crucial component of sustainable living. By switching to renewable energy sources like hydropower, wind, and solar, greenhouse gas emissions and reliance on fossil fuels can be significantly reduced. Implementing energy-efficient measures in homes and workplaces, such as installing energy-efficient appliances, upgrading insulation, and utilizing programmable thermostats, further reduces energy usage and utility costs. Communities and people can promote resilience and energy independence while simultaneously reducing climate change by prioritizing renewable energy and energy efficiency.

Sustainable living includes cutting back on consumption and switching to renewable energy sources, preserving natural ecosystems, and fostering biodiversity. Maintaining thriving ecosystems and guaranteeing the survival of various plant and animal species depend on biodiversity conservation. By establishing wildlife habitats, planting native plants in their gardens, and supporting the preservation of natural areas like forests, wetlands, and marine environments, people can contribute to biodiversity conservation. We can maintain ecosystem services critical to human well-being and the world's health, such as pollination, water purification, and carbon sequestration, by safeguarding biodiversity.

Moreover, ethical and conscientious consumption decisions that prioritize fair labor standards, social justice, and animal welfare are also part of sustainable living. Customers may support social equality and environmental justice by patronizing businesses and brands that maintain ethical standards and treat employees, communities, and animals with dignity. Reducing meat intake or switching to plant-based diets can also significantly impact the environment by lowering greenhouse gas emissions, using less water, and reducing the amount of forest cleared for cattle grazing and feed. Selecting fair trade, organic, and locally grown goods can also promote sustainable agricultural methods and lessen the adverse effects of food production and distribution on the environment and society.

In addition to individual efforts, sustainable living calls for structural change and group efforts to solve social and environmental issues. This can involve endorsing laws and programs that support conservation, renewable energy, and sustainable development on a local, national, and international scale. Participating in grassroots movements, supporting environmentally conscious companies and organizations, and becoming involved in community action can all help build on individual efforts and bring about significant change toward a more just and sustainable future.

Adopting eco-friendly and sustainable lifestyles is critical to maintaining the planet's health and guaranteeing future generations' prosperity. People can make a big difference in tackling environmental and social issues and creating a more sustainable society by cutting back on consumption, using less energy, preserving biodiversity, encouraging ethical consumption, and pushing for systemic change. In the end, sustainable living is about promoting a shared commitment to responsible stewardship of the Earth and its inhabitants, not just about adopting personal lifestyle decisions.

## Mindfulness and gratitude practices

Practicing mindfulness and appreciation provides daily practical tools to cultivate resilience, happiness, and inner peace. These practices, which have their roots in age-old wisdom traditions and are backed by contemporary scientific study, are becoming increasingly well-known for their capacity to improve well-being and foster a closer connection with others and the environment. Mindfulness invites us to build awareness of our thoughts, feelings, and sensations without passing judgment. It is commonly defined as the discipline of paying attention to the present moment with openness, curiosity, and acceptance. By engaging in mindfulness practices, we can improve our mental clarity, insight, and emotional control, which will enable us to face life's obstacles with more knowledge and composure.

Contrarily, practicing gratitude is the act of recognizing and appreciating life's benefits, gifts, and positive features. To cultivate thankfulness, we must consciously direct our attention toward the things we are grateful for, no matter how tiny, and express our appreciation for the abundance and beauty that exist all around us. According to research, cultivating gratitude can significantly impact our physical and mental health, increasing resilience, happiness, and general well-being. Moreover, gratitude encourages a change in viewpoint, enabling us to see past our current problems and realize how linked everything is.

Practices of thankfulness and mindfulness can be combined to increase their effects and profoundly improve our lives. To truly savor and appreciate the times of joy and plenty in our lives, mindful gratitude entails bringing focused awareness to the experience of appreciation itself. This can be as easy as taking a moment to appreciate the kindness of a stranger, the beauty of a sunset, or the warmth of a loved one's smile. By paying close attention to them, we can enhance the beneficial impacts of these instances of thankfulness on our disposition, state of mind, and general well-being.

Furthermore, practicing mindfulness might increase our ability to be grateful by fostering a stronger feeling of awareness and presence in our day-to-day activities. By approaching every moment with mindfulness, we can fully appreciate the wonder and beauty of life by becoming more alert to the richness and complexity of our experiences. This increased awareness can result in a greater sense of thankfulness for all the blessings in our lives—from the air we breathe to the relationships that support and nurture us.

We can handle life's inevitable obstacles with more grace and resilience when we practice mindfulness and appreciation. We can increase our ability to remain present with challenging feelings and situations without getting overwhelmed or reacting by practicing mindfulness. This keeps us from becoming overwhelmed by fear, rage, or despair and enables us to respond to adversity with greater clarity, compassion, and resilience. Furthermore, practicing thankfulness can assist us in reframing how we view misfortune, allowing us to find progress, purpose, and even beauty in the midst of it all.

Incorporating mindfulness and appreciation practices into our daily lives can be accessible yet compelling. This can involve scheduling regular periods for formal meditation or introspection and integrating mindfulness and gratitude into routine tasks like walking, eating, or socializing. Through the practice of mindfulness and gratitude, we can develop a more profound sense of connection, joy, and presence in each instant of our existence. In the end, gratitude and mindfulness exercises provide effective routes to increased fulfillment, resilience, and well-being, enabling us to navigate the intricacies of contemporary life with more ease and grace.

# CHAPTER XIV

# Community and Solitary Practice

## Joining a coven vs. solitary practice

Whether to practice Wicca alone or in a coven is a very personal choice based on individual tastes, convictions, and spiritual requirements. Both strategies have advantages and disadvantages, and a person's Wiccan path can be significantly impacted by their decision to practice alone or join a coven.

Practitioners can experience a sense of belonging, support, and companionship by joining a coven. Covens are usually small gatherings of Wiccans that gather to learn the craft, celebrate rituals, and give mutual support to one another's spiritual journeys. Joining a coven enables practitioners to take part in group rituals and ceremonies that can strengthen their connection to the divine and the larger Wiccan community, as well as learn from seasoned mentors and elders and receive advice and criticism on their work. Furthermore, covens frequently offer chances for companionship, social engagement, and joint study of Wiccan doctrine and customs.

Additionally, becoming a member of a coven can offer a disciplined and planned method of practicing Wicca. Generally speaking, covens have set rituals, customs, and rules that offer a structure for spiritual development. This structure provides clear guidance and support in negotiating the complexity of the craft, making it especially helpful for novices or those looking for a more organized approach to Wicca. Being a part of a coven can also offer possibilities for personal growth and transformation through group rituals, initiations, and other rites of passage, as well as accountability and a desire to maintain a regular spiritual practice.

But becoming a part of a coven has its restrictions and difficulties. Covens are made up of people with a variety of personalities, experiences, and worldviews. Hence, disputes and conflicts may occur among the members. Furthermore, covens could have particular standards or demands of its members, such as attending regularly scheduled meetings, participating in group activities, or abiding by predetermined laws or regulations. For those with demanding schedules, competing obligations, or a desire for more independence in their spiritual practice, this may be difficult. Furthermore, it might be challenging to locate a coven that shares one's ideas, values, and spiritual objectives, especially in places with tiny or dispersed Wiccan populations.

Nonetheless, solo Wicca practice allows one a higher level of independence, flexibility, and autonomy. Without the limitations and expectations of a group, solitary practitioners are free to follow their spiritual path at their leisure. This enables people to customize their practice to suit their tastes, requirements, and interests by combining aspects of other customs, rituals, and teachings that speak to them on a personal level. Since solitary practitioners are encouraged to create customs, meditations, and practices that uniquely represent their connection to the divine, they can also offer possibilities for profound introspection, self-discovery, and spiritual growth.

Sitting alone can also be very helpful for people who value seclusion, privacy, or a more reflective approach to spirituality. Without the constraints or distractions of group dynamics, solitary practitioners can carry out their solitary rituals, meditations, and spiritual practices in the privacy of their own homes or natural surroundings. Since solitary practice provides for a profound, intimate connection to the divine and the natural world, this can be especially relevant for introverted people or those who find inspiration and refuge in nature.

But practicing alone has its drawbacks and difficulties as well. Solitary practitioners may experience feelings of isolation or disconnection from the larger Wiccan community in the absence of the support and direction of a coven, especially if they are unable to access nearby pagan organizations or resources. Additionally, since solitary practitioners are responsible for their spiritual development and progress without the accountability or structure of a group, they must possess a higher level of self-discipline, motivation, and self-reliance. Beginners or those who yearn for the approval of others, social engagement, or validation that comes from being a part of a community may find this problematic.

In conclusion, the option to practice alone or join a coven is highly subjective and based on personal tastes, convictions, and spiritual requirements. Each strategy has advantages and disadvantages of its own, and what works best for one individual might not work best for another. Respecting the sacredness of all life, developing a solid and genuine connection to the divine, and accepting one's spiritual path are more important than joining a coven or going solo.

## Building a supportive community

Creating an encouraging group is crucial to helping us develop resilience, connection, and belonging. Supportive communities provide a sense of camaraderie, mutual aid, and solidarity that enhances our lives and promotes our sense of well-being. These communities can take many forms, such as close-knit friendship groups, local neighborhood associations, or online networks of like-minded people. A supportive community where people come together to encourage and uplift one another through life's ups and downs is fundamentally based on trust, empathy, and mutual respect. We can establish environments where everyone feels appreciated, heard, and supported by establishing solid relationships, encouraging honest communication, and a culture of gratitude and compassion.

The sense of connection and belonging that a supportive community fosters is one of its main advantages. A feeling of identity and purpose, as well as chances for friendship, social engagement, and shared experiences, are provided by belonging to a community. We can feel seen, heard, and understood by people who share our values, interests, and experiences when we are part of a supportive community, whether through sharing laughter and conversation, grieving milestones, or just hanging out and chatting. Our mental and emotional health depends on having a sense of belonging since it protects us against isolation, loneliness, and the stressors of everyday life.

Furthermore, helpful groups provide tools and advice that might make it easier for people to deal with life's obstacles. A safety net of support and solidarity that may make all the difference during trying times is provided by supportive communities, whether it is through lending a helping hand, listening intently, or providing practical aid when needed. People may overcome challenges, develop resilience, and flourish in the face of adversity with the support of a loving community, which might range from helping with home tasks to offering emotional support during times of crisis.

Creating an encouraging community also helps cultivate a culture of teamwork, cooperation, and collective effort, all of which can result in constructive societal change. When communities unite behind shared values, aspirations, and goals, they can mobilize resources, lobby for change, and work toward common goals that benefit everyone. To bring about significant change and improve the world for the coming generations, supportive communities must actively promote social justice, environmental preservation, and community growth.

All members must, however, consciously make an effort, be committed, and invest in creating a supportive community. It entails establishing inviting, inclusive, and secure areas for everyone, irrespective of background, identity, or religious convictions. It also calls for encouraging honest dialogue, finding positive solutions to disagreements, and acting with compassion and empathy for others. Building a supportive group takes time, patience, and persistence, but the benefits of connecting with like-minded people who encourage and support one another are priceless.

In summary, developing a community of support is critical to promoting resilience, connection, and belonging in our lives. In addition to providing chances for cooperation and group action, supportive communities also give a feeling of community, enhancing our quality of life. We can establish environments where everyone feels appreciated, heard, and supported by establishing solid relationships, encouraging honest communication, and a culture of gratitude and compassion. In the end, having a supportive community is more than just helping ourselves; it's about uniting to encourage and support one another, making the world a better place for everybody.


## Online resources and networks

Online resources and networks are essential in today's interconnected society because they enable worldwide communication, cooperation, and information access. The internet provides many tools and avenues for people to interact, acquire knowledge, and develop their careers, ranging from social media sites and online discussion boards to scholarly portals and business networking sites. Online resources and networks have revolutionized communication, knowledge sharing, and community building. People can now interact with like-minded others regardless of distance or physical proximity, sharing their interests, hobbies, and ambitions.

The ease of use and accessibility of internet networks and resources is one of their main advantages. People can access a wealth of knowledge, resources, and skills on almost any subject by clicking a few buttons. With the internet, we have access to many resources that can be used for anything from learning a new skill to exploring potential hobbies to asking friends and family for advice. People can learn at their own pace and on their own time by using free or inexpensive educational materials on websites like Coursera, Khan Academy, and YouTube. Furthermore, social media groups and online forums allow people to meet people who share their interests, exchange questions and have conversations about anything from pop culture and technology to pop culture and health.

Furthermore, Internet networks and services for individuals and groups make global communication and cooperation easier. People can connect with friends, family, and coworkers on social networking sites like Facebook, Twitter, and Instagram. They can also exchange updates and images and maintain real-time communication. People can build their professional networks, connect with mentors, employers, and collaborators, and access career information and job prospects using professional networking sites like LinkedIn. Additionally, teams and individuals may work remotely, share files and documents, and work together in real-time on projects regardless of where they are, thanks to online collaboration platforms like Google Docs, Dropbox, and Slack.

Online tools and networks have also made it easier for people to acquire information and expertise, enabling them to develop personally and follow their passions. Through online educational venues like TED Talks, podcasts, and webinars, people can learn from top experts and thought leaders in various sectors, from science and technology to the arts and culture. Furthermore, many books, papers, and research materials that were formerly only accessible to people with access to physical libraries or academic institutions are now made available to everyone through online libraries and digital archives. Online resources and networks have leveled the playing field and created new chances for people to follow their interests and accomplish their goals by democratizing access to knowledge.

However, Online networks and services can also have disadvantages, such as issues with misinformation, privacy, and security. Concerns over personal data security and privacy, as well as the dissemination of false information and fake news, have been brought up by the growth of social media platforms and online communities. Furthermore, the popularity of online echo chambers and filter bubbles can restrict exposure to various ideas and viewpoints and reinforce preexisting biases. Furthermore, for many people, especially those in impoverished communities or developing nations, the digital divide—the difference between those who have access to digital technologies and those who do not— remains a significant obstacle to using online resources and networks.

In conclusion, internet tools and networks have completely changed how we interact, learn, and communicate with one another. They have also given people access to a never-before-seen range of information, communities, and possibilities to follow their hobbies. An abundance of resources and chances for people to interact, learn, and grow can be found online, ranging from social media networks and educational platforms to professional networking sites and online collaboration tools. However, Online networks and services can also have disadvantages, such as issues with misinformation, privacy, and security. It will be crucial to solve these issues in the future while utilizing the promise of online networks and resources to build a more inclusive, connected, and knowledgeable society for everybody.

# CONCLUSION

"Unlocking Wiccan Mysteries and Spirituality: Sacred Whispers: Embracing the Mysticism and Spiritual Practices of Wicca" offers a profound journey into the heart of Wiccan spirituality, inviting readers to explore the rich tapestry of mystical teachings, rituals, and practices that comprise this ancient and sacred tradition. Through insightful guidance, practical exercises, and inspiring anecdotes, the book illuminates the path of Wicca, guiding readers on a transformative journey of self-discovery, empowerment, and spiritual growth.

From honoring the cycles of nature and communing with the divine to harnessing the power of magic and cultivating mindfulness and gratitude, "Sacred Whispers" offers a comprehensive roadmap for embracing the mysteries of Wicca and deepening one's connection to the sacred within and without.

As readers delve into the pages of "Sacred Whispers," they are invited to embark on a journey of exploration and awakening, discovering the hidden wisdom and magic at the heart of Wiccan spirituality. Through engaging storytelling, practical exercises, and profound insights, the book empowers readers to unlock the mysteries of Wicca and embrace their unique spiritual path. Whether new to Wicca or seasoned practitioners, readers will find "Sacred Whispers" a valuable resource for deepening their understanding of Wiccan spirituality and enriching their spiritual practice. With its empowering message of self-discovery, connection, and transformation, "Sacred Whispers" will inspire and uplift readers on their journey of spiritual awakening and growth.